PRAISE FOR *REVERS*

"Andrew has done it again! First he nudged us toward lucidity in the sleep bardo with his awesome book *Dream Yoga*. Then toward more lucidity in the life bardo with the even more awesome *Dreams of Light*. Now he brilliantly demonstrates how there need be no gaps, even when we confront the untoward, when we are jarred out of positive awareness by adversity and pain and injury, and we turn it all into advantage in his latest great work, this wonderful *Reverse Meditation*. I cannot recommend it highly enough—a great read and immensely useful for thriving and evolving positively in this world of obstacles."

ROBERT THURMAN
professor emeritus, author of *Wisdom Is Bliss* and the Bantam
Books translation of The Tibetan Book of the Dead

"*Reverse Meditation* is a brilliant masterpiece that illustrates that Andrew Holecek's extensive exploration of inner space has given him a unique perspective of outer space. Andrew understands that each and every one of us is in space at this very moment. Not only are we all traveling through the Universe on this spaceship that we call Earth, but we also generate the illusion of solid ground through our individual egos. Andrew clearly demonstrates that many of the problems we all face can be traced to our futile attempts to give our egos a place to stand. Through reverse meditation, we can mold ourselves into the softest, most open, yet strongest and most indestructible thing in the Universe—space itself. Nothing can hurt space! A must-read for anyone who wants to improve their life and expand their horizons."

RON GARAN
former NASA astronaut, author of *Floating in Darkness*

"Meditation sometimes becomes dualistic: we learn to let go of thoughts and feelings, to cultivate an empty mind. What do we lose when we split ourselves like that? What might we realize if, instead of contracting in the face of pain and other unwanted experience, we open up to them—realize our nonduality with them? *Reverse Meditation* shows us how to do that and how it can transform our lives."

DAVID R. LOY
author of *Money, Sex, War, Karma*

REVERSE
MEDITATION

ALSO BY ANDREW HOLECEK

BOOKS

Dream Yoga: Illuminating Your Life Through Lucid Dreaming and the Tibetan Yogas of Sleep

Dreams of Light: The Profound Daytime Practice of Lucid Dreaming

The Lucid Dreaming Workbook: A Step-by-Step Guide to Mastering Your Dream Life

Meditation in the iGeneration: How to Meditate in a World of Speed and Stress

The Power and the Pain: Transforming Spiritual Hardship into Joy

Preparing to Die: Practical Advice and Spiritual Wisdom from the Tibetan Buddhist Tradition

AUDIO PROGRAM

Dream Yoga: The Tibetan Path of Awakening Through Lucid Dreaming

REVERSE MEDITATION

How to Use Your Pain and
Most Difficult Emotions as the
Doorway to Inner Freedom

ANDREW HOLECEK

sounds true
BOULDER, COLORADO

Sounds True
Boulder, CO 80306

This book is not intended as a substitute for the medical recommendations of physicians,
mental health professionals, or other health-care providers. Rather, it is intended to offer
information to help the reader cooperate with physicians, mental health professionals,
and health-care providers in a mutual quest for optimal well-being. We advise readers to
carefully review and understand the ideas presented and to seek the advice of a qualified
professional before attempting to use them.

Published 2023

Cover design by Jennifer Miles
Book design by Ranee Kahler

Excerpts from *Spiritual Bypassing: When Spirituality Disconnects Us from What Really
Matters* by Robert Augustus Masters, published by North Atlantic Books, copyright ©
2010 Robert Augustus Masters. Reprinted by permission of North Atlantic Books.

Printed in Canada

BK06693

Library of Congress Cataloging-in-Publication Data
Names: Holecek, Andrew, 1955- author.
Title: Reverse meditation : how to use your pain and most difficult
emotions as the doorway to inner freedom / Andrew Holecek.
Description: Boulder, CO : Sounds True, [2023]
Identifiers: LCCN 2022051667 (print) | LCCN 2022051668 (ebook) |
    ISBN 9781649631053 (paperback) | ISBN 9781649631060 (ebook)
Subjects: LCSH: Meditation. | Pain. | Suffering. | Meditation--Buddhism. |
Pain--Religious aspects--Buddhism. | Suffering--Religious aspects--Buddhism.
Classification: LCC BL627 .H63 2023 (print) | LCC BL627 (ebook) |
    DDC 204/.35--dc23/eng/20230221
LC record available at https://lccn.loc.gov/2022051667
LC ebook record available at https://lccn.loc.gov/2022051668

MIX
Paper from
responsible sources
FSC® C016245

10 9 8 7 6 5 4 3 2 1

In loving memory of Taylor Christine Holecek-McDonald
and Stephen Owen Mathews

We would rather be ruined than changed,
We would rather die in our dread
Than climb the cross of the moment
And let our illusions die.

—W. H. AUDEN

A monk said to Dongshan, "Cold and heat descend upon us.
  How can we avoid them?"
Dongshan said, "Why don't you go where there is no cold
  or heat?"
The monk said, "Where is the place where there is no cold
  or heat?"
Dongshan said, "When cold, let it be so cold that it kills
  you; when hot, let it be so hot that it kills you."

—BLUE CLIFF RECORD, CASE 43 KOAN

CONTENTS

INTRODUCTION

The greatest gift has been a complete reversal in my
understanding of the workings of the universe. . . . Such a
reversal is cause for great optimism because this fundamental
shift in worldview allows us to stake out a far grander
role in determining the evolution of this universe.

—EBEN ALEXANDER

I came to understand heaven and hell in a new way. In
a striking reversal of perspective, I saw that hell was
not the opposite of heaven, as is usually taught, but
the guardian companion of divine realization.

—CHRISTOPHER BACHE

Meditation has found a home in the West. Countless scientific studies tout its benefits, and a multitude of students proclaim its life-changing value. I am one of those students. For over forty-five years I have practiced this ancient art, and I continue to reap its remarkable rewards. While I remain a follower of many wisdom traditions, and believe that no one has a patent on truth, thirty years ago I took refuge in Buddhism. The adage "Chase two rabbits; catch none" points out the necessity of commitment, and the dangers of spreading yourself too thin.

My passion for meditation led me into the traditional Tibetan three-year retreat, where I became a monk with robes and a shaved head, meditating fourteen hours a day in a remote monastery. I even slept sitting up in meditation posture, practicing the nocturnal meditations of dream and sleep yoga. Three-year retreat is like a meditation university, providing the opportunity to practice dozens of meditations in the most nurturing environment. It remains the most transformative experience of my life.

Of the many practices I was introduced to in retreat, one meditation stands out: the quirky, intense, multifaceted, and revolutionary practice of *reverse meditation*. I learned these practices within the context of Mahāmudrā (Sanskrit for "great seal"), a lofty tradition in Tibetan Buddhism that explores the nature of the mind.[1] This was over twenty years ago, and since then these radical meditations have become a cornerstone of my spiritual path.

They're called "reverse" meditation for a number of reasons. First, these practices are the opposite, or reverse, of what many of us associate with meditation. Most people think that meditation is about feeling good, getting "Zen," or otherwise chilling out. But this is just one small aspect of meditation. Complete meditation is not about feeling good—it's about getting real. And getting real requires dealing with the reality of difficult situations.

Second, these unique meditations are designed to reverse our relationship to unwanted experiences, which means going directly into them instead of avoiding them. In so doing we can discover the *basic goodness* of whatever arises, which is deeper than interpretative goodness. Basic goodness refers to the ineffable "suchness, isness, thatness" of whatever occurs—good or bad.

If we capitulate to our usual avoidance strategies, we push the acute, conscious psychological discomfort of avoidance into becoming a chronic, unconscious mental cramp. The discomfort is still there, but now it's buried deep in our body-mind matrix, where it works backstage to dictate much of our onstage life. The rejected experience then manifests symptomatically—it becomes an undiagnosed reflection of an underlying discord that expresses itself in virtually everything we do. Our actions then become evasion tactics—reactivity, psychological duress, physical illness, and all manner of unskillful responses to the challenges of life—as we try to skirt these buried, uncomfortable feelings.

The reverse meditations give us the opportunity to relate *to* our mind instead of *from* it—and also to establish a relationship to our evasion tactics, which otherwise become obstacles that act like scar tissue to sequester the unwanted experience from consciousness. Relating *from* our mind, from our reactivity, is no relationship at all. In place of conscious relationship, we respond with knee-jerk reflexes to difficult experience, a reactivity that kicks us out of our feeling body and into our thinking head, and into unnecessary suffering. Instead of dealing authentically with the challenging somatic sensation, we leap into inauthentic conceptual proliferation (confabulating and catastrophizing) to buffer ourselves from the discomfort of our feelings. We run from the honest pain and real news that come with being human, and into dishonest commentary and fake news. The truth is that many of the worst things in our life are things that never really "happened"!

Third, the reverse meditations upend our sense of meditation altogether. They represent a revolution in spiritual practice that turns our understanding of meditation inside out and upside down, and therefore radically expand our practice. Situations that were once antithetical to meditation now *become* our meditation. Obstacles that previously obstructed our spiritual path now become our path. This means that everything becomes our meditation. Nothing is forbidden. We can enter lifetime retreat in the midst of ordinary life.

DOWN AND DIRTY

Because the reverse meditations invite unwanted experiences, they're no day at the beach. (Unless you expand your notion of "beach.") Many spiritual practitioners enter the path because they're looking for peace and happiness. The contemporary teacher A. H. Almaas, founder of the Diamond Way, writes, "When most people set out on the spiritual path they're unwittingly setting out for heaven."[2] One limitation of conventional understandings of meditation is the "feel good" agenda. Meditation then slips into the standard comfort plan. If it's not going to make me feel better, why bother? What's the point? That agenda is viable, but incomplete. We all want to feel good. But where does your meditation go when things go bad? Where is your spirituality when "rock meets bone," as they say in Tibet?

The reverse meditations make you feel better, even when the crap hits the fan and things feel bad. They do so by expanding your sense of what "better" and "bad" truly mean. You really can feel good under *any* circumstance; you just need to enlarge your sense of goodness and refine your understanding of "bad." Your comfort plan can evolve to encompass even the most uncomfortable experiences. The meditation master Milarepa, who spent twelve years in intensive retreat and dealt with legendary hardship, sang:

> When I get a lot of stuff coming up I feel extremely well
> When the highs roll into lows feels even better still
> When confusion gets complicated I feel extremely well
> Fearsome visions get worse and worse feels even better still
> The suffering being bliss feels so good that feeling bad
>   feels good.[3]

Feeling bad feels good? Suffering becomes bliss? Is this some twisted form of spiritual masochism? How is it possible to relate to hardship in this way? By reversing your relationship. By discovering the peace that lies within the pain.

"Reverse" meditations are counterinstinctual, counterintuitive, and counter to our normal versions of conditional happiness. They go against the grain of our comfort plan. But these unusual meditations lead to the discovery of unconditional happiness—the tranquil beach that lies within the most turbulent situations. Even if a tidal wave slams into your life, you are now equipped to ride that surf. You'll be able to find your way to that endless tranquil beach no matter where you are and what you're going through.

In other words, by putting your meditation into reverse you'll actually find yourself going forward. Stepping into your pain allows for stepping up your evolution. These unusual practices accelerate your path by bringing everything onto it. Serious meditators often go into retreat, even conventionally, in order to advance. But this book will demonstrate that you don't need to sit in tranquility on a meditation cushion, or escape into a retreat cabin, to meditate. Just reverse your rendering of meditation, and realize you have the goods to chill out in a blast furnace.

My teacher Khenpo Tsültrim Gyamtso Rinpoche advised his students, "Nurture your meditation by destroying it." What he meant is destroy your contracted understanding of meditation. Don't limit yourself. If you continue to separate meditation from the hardships of life, you end up limiting both meditation and life.

The reverse meditations are earthy, gritty, and very real. At times they will slam your heavenly versions of spirituality smack into the earth and almost force you to mix dirt with divinity. These practices turn the notion of spirituality on its head. Instead of "waking up," it's more about "waking down." Instead of transcendence, it's more about "subscendence." Instead of trying to get out, it's more about getting in.

This rebellious view often creates a whiplash effect because of its impact. It's such a sweeping reversal of traditional notions of meditation and spirituality. And the practices that lead to the incorporation of this unusual path can be similarly jarring. But so is life. You have to be intrepid to walk this path. It's worth the price of admission because these practices are your ticket into reality. They allow you to find the spiritual in the material—in the good, the bad, and the ugly—and annihilate the notion of "path" altogether. In the end, you're not going anywhere. This converse path will lead you back into the real world, back into the difficulties you were attempting to flee. They will help you find freedom in precisely what you were trying to avoid.

CONTRACTION

Over the past forty-five years of studying the great wisdom traditions, I have searched for the irreducible factors behind suffering. What are the common denominators behind samsāra (the Sanskrit word for conditional reality) and all its hardship? Can these denominators themselves be further reduced into a foundational tenet? Henry David Thoreau captures this longing to deeply understand the world:

> I went to the woods because I wished to live deliberately, to front only the essential facts of life, and see if I could not learn what it had to teach, and not, when I came to die, discover that I had not lived. I did not wish to live what was not life, living is so dear; nor did I wish to practice resignation, unless it was quite necessary. I wanted to live deep and suck out all the marrow of life, to live so sturdily and Spartan-like as to put to rout all that was not life, to cut a broad swath and shave close, to drive life into a corner, and reduce it to its lowest terms.[4]

All my meditation retreats have been "to drive life into a corner, and reduce it to its lowest terms." One common denominator has slowly but consistently emerged as the central player behind all my pain. *Contraction.*

Contraction is a principle that I will be using to describe the evasion tactics, the reactivity, the self-generated obstacles that stand between us and inner freedom. Later chapters will outline this principle more fully, but for now we can just say that contraction is the retreat from reality that typically happens when things start to hurt.

The Kabbalistic tradition uses the term *tzimtzum*, also translated as "withdrawal," for this principle of contraction. With every contraction, we withdraw from what's happening, from authentic contact with reality, and into our inauthentic storylines about it. But bona fide spirituality is a contact sport. You have to be willing to get hit. If you relate to the contact properly, you will be hit with the truth, and eventually with reality. The Jewish scholar Zvi Ish-Shalom gives us a sense of the profundity of the contraction principle:

> Contraction also represents the movement of the infinite light, the light of *Ein Sof* ["no-end, infinite"], into the

manifestation of form, until its eventual presentation as the dualistic human experience of separation.

When we understand this process we can trace it back, we can follow the experience of embodied form . . . back through all the dimensions of light; this process of repeated contraction and expansion birthed into being, from the most coarse and material into the most subtle and ethereal.

. . . [E]very individual life, with all of our suffering and all of our contractions, is the potential of the infinite expressing itself.[5]

This is a thick statement that we will unpack in later chapters. In simpler terms: like Hansel and Gretel in the fairy tale, we can follow the breadcrumbs (of contraction) back home. Tracing the reiterative process of contraction back to our true nature, we find our way to things as they really are before we withdraw. Ish-Shalom continues, "Suffering, or contraction, is simply the mistaken perception that we are a separate entity, defined by our self concept. . . . When this property of light is contracted in our human experience, knowledge of who and what we are escapes us."[6] And we forget. The reverse meditations are meditations of remembering—or re-membering, taking us back home. Starting right where we are, with our reactivity and resistance toward unwanted emotions and experiences, through reverse meditation we can work our way back to the source of our discomfort and dissatisfaction—to the very subtle primordial contraction that generates our sense of self.

The reverse meditations allow us to transform obstacle (contraction) into opportunity (openness). Expansion and contraction, together, are a combustion cycle that drives the path forward—or, in our journey, "backward." Understanding this will show us how to treasure our contractions as necessary fuel for the path. Like the beating of our heart, we need contraction to allow for expansion.

The reverse meditations and contraction relate to each other in the following way: if we give in to our habits of avoiding discomfort, we transform conscious pain (mostly emotional and psychological) into unconscious cramps. Never do we contract with such rapidity and ferocity than when we're in pain. We instinctively contract away from unwanted experience, a reactivity that may temporarily remove us from acute pain, but that ironically ensures chronic suffering. Pain and suffering are not the same. Suffering is an inappropriate relationship to pain. And by reversing that relationship, we can relieve our suffering. The reverse meditations equip us with the tools to reorder our relationship to contraction by opening to it, transforming contraction into relaxation, closure into openness, and agony into a new understanding of ecstasy.

In so doing, the reverse meditations also heal the fracture of duality (explored in chapter 13)—the birth of the illusion of self and other that is born from these reiterative contractions, a fracturing that is at the root of all our suffering. Our journey will therefore lead to an open, honest, and nondual relationship to reality, which includes pain. The reverse meditations enable you to become one with your pain, and embrace it rather than brace against it, which magically liberates both you and the pain. The pain is gone. And so are "you." What's left? What remains after this nondual embrace? Even the one becomes none. No-thing is left. Emptiness is left, which is equivalent to a radiant fullness—and a blazing new experience of life. Just what that is will be revealed in the pages ahead.

This book is therefore not just a practice manual, but a repair manual—an owner's guide to the difficulties of life. The ideas here present a profound way to repair our relationship to unwanted experiences by reversing the way we deal with them. *Reverse Meditation* is fundamentally a way to realize unconditional happiness, by pointing out the unnecessary ways we make ourselves and others miserable.

WHY ME?

As a former dental surgeon, I have spent decades in the pain business. I'm acutely aware of the clinical aspects of intense pain, the pathophysiology of neurological transmission, and the necessity of pain management with standard regimens, including drugs. I have written thousands of prescriptions for pain medication, and countless more for anti-anxiety agents (which amount to anti-contraction agents.) I'm not writing this book from an ivory tower. The practices I'm offering come from the trenches on the front lines of life.

As an author in the field of thanatology (death and dying), as well as the shadow sides of soteriology (the doctrine of salvation), I have wide-ranging experience in the academic and clinical sides of psychological and emotional suffering.[7] But mostly, I'm just like you. I live in a world that can be extraordinarily painful. In this divisive and contentious age, the pain just seems to be getting worse. Every time I turn on the news, I see more anguish in the world. My heart has been broken; my guts sometimes feel like they have been ripped out. The reverse meditations have become a faithful friend I can always count on. A friend that walks with me as I travel along the bumpy road of life, forever ready to lend a healing hand.

HOW TO USE THIS BOOK

Meditation is not one practice, just like sport is not merely one activity. There are as many meditations as there are sports, and we will explore a progression of meditation practices, building and refining upon their predecessors. The reverse meditations are radical—we'll be working our way up to them. If you find the way gets a bit steep in part 1, jump ahead to the meditations in part 2 to start bringing the material into your life, and to take a break. Parts 1 and 2 bootstrap each other, so feel free to dance between these two sections. The numerous endnotes support the journey for deeper divers, but can be skipped, or left for a second reading.

Three core meditations form the axis of this book: the baseline practice of mindfulness (more specifically, referential meditation, in chapter 7), which matures into the practice of open awareness (the nonreferential meditations, chapters 8 and 9), which prepares you for the reverse meditations (chapters 10, 11, and 12). Interlaced with these core meditations are a number of contemplations and "meditation snacks," practices designed to be used on the spot in difficult situations.

We'll generate stability with the three core practices, and applicability with the contemplations and meditation snacks.

Together, the contemplations and meditations offered in this book will allow you to slowly unravel the numerous knots you have tied yourself into, release the contractions felt as the underlying tension of your life, and will culminate in a deep sense of ease, even when life is filled with dis-ease. The layers of contraction will be pointed out one by one, then opened with correlative meditations, releasing vast stores of energy trapped inside. The result is invigorating, liberating, and ultimately enlightening.

But the process that leads to this freedom, the fundamental awakening and return to life, is not itself always blissful. It's similar to when your foot has fallen sound asleep—it feels like pins and needles as it wakes up. If your hand is frozen stiff on a winter day, it can burn like hell when it thaws. With the right view, however, you willingly endure the discomfort necessary to wake up, because you know that the energy and freedom released by dropping your resistance, and walking the peaceful path of inner disarmament, is worth it.

PART 1

THE BASICS

CHAPTER 1

RIGHT VIEW

When the whole thing's just not working, everything's
  lined up against you,
Don't try to find some way to change it all;
Here, the point to make your practice is reverse the
  way you see it,
Don't try to make it stop or to improve.
Adverse conditions happen, when they do it's so delightful—
They make a little song of sheer delight!

—GOTSANGPA (MEDITATION MASTER)

Two central challenges await those who are willing to explore the path
of reverse meditations and work with the self-generated obstacles, or
"contractions," that occur as a way to avoid painful or uncomfortable feelings.
The first challenge is the conscious discomfort that accompanies this
path. (The second is the subtle, ubiquitous, and unconscious dimensions
of contraction, a central idea that is explored in chapter 3.) Contraction
originally occurred, and continues to occur, as a way to avoid uncomfortable
feelings. But that discomfort doesn't just disappear if you withdraw from the
experience. It becomes embodied in the contraction itself, which throws the
discord into your unconscious mind, and eventually into your body. From
there it festers, like a psychic cyst leaking toxins into your life. The cyst needs
to be surgically incised and drained, and that isn't always pleasant.

Reverse meditation is a kind of psychic surgery that can excise your self-generated obstacles, drain your resistance, but it requires a willingness to face painful or uncomfortable feelings. The idea of tolerating difficult situations and dissatisfaction as a means to end suffering may seem paradoxical and hard to follow. But reverse meditation is in harmony with the Buddhist teachings of *right view*, the first and most important factor of the Noble Eightfold Path that leads to the end of suffering.[1] In this context, "view" is akin to philosophy or outlook. It points us in the right direction and keeps us from losing our way.

From a conventional perspective, the right view that informs our journey is so contrary to traditional approaches that *the view is itself a reverse view*. It's the opposite of how we've been taught to relate to reality—let alone unwanted experience. The view is simple to state but not easy to actualize: Whatever arises in mind or reality is sacred. It might not arise as your version of perfection or sanctity, but the nature of all phenomena is utterly divine. And that includes you—and your pain.

For many of us, the right view comes across as just wrong. But throughout time and across traditions, wisdom seekers have discovered that the extraordinary claim of right view—that everything is perfect, just as it is—is fundamentally liberating for those who are willing to embrace its extraordinary evidence. In present-day terms, the neuroanatomist Jill Bolte Taylor is describing right view in recounting her experience of the "shifted perception" caused by a stroke: "It was impossible for me," she says, "to perceive either physical or emotional loss because I was not capable of experiencing separation or individuality. . . . In the absence of my left hemisphere's negative judgment, I perceived myself as perfect, whole, and beautiful just the way I was."[2] And we also find the view of perfect purity as central to the ancient teachings of the Great Perfection, or Dzogchen, of Tibetan Buddhism: "Everything is naturally perfect just as it is, completely pure and undefiled," explain the twentieth-century teachers Chögyam Trungpa Rinpoche and Rigdzin Shikpo. "One should never think of oneself as 'sinful' or worthless, but as naturally pure and perfect, lacking nothing."[3]

The same view is echoed in the doctrine of "basic goodness" in the Shambhala tradition (founded by Trungpa Rinpoche):

> At the most basic level of our being, we have everything we need to celebrate our lives on this planet. . . . The basic goodness of our world is not the "good" side of a world divided into good and bad. When we divide the world in that way—even in our minds—we automatically put conditions on everything around us so that it is good if it fulfills our conditions and bad if it does not. Basic goodness is unconditioned . . . [it] has nothing to do with "feeling good."[4]

The Asian wisdom traditions proclaim their versions of basic goodness, lending their voices to a view so contrary to limited Western views. Gurumayi Chidvilasananda describes right view in a poem that takes its language from the Hindu tradition of nondual Shaiva Tantra:

> Where has my ecstasy brought me?
> It has brought me to a place
> Where nothing is left but the pure "I,"
> Pūrṇāham-vimarśa, the perfect "I"-consciousness.
> Now that I know what my existence is all about:
> Nothing remains but the ecstasy of my true Self.[5]

The ancient Taoist philosopher Chuang Tzu taught, "In the state of pure experience, what is known as the union of the individual with the whole is reached," a state of experience that reflects the perfect knowledge of the ancients, in which "there is nothing but the one, the whole" and to which "nothing can be added."[6] And in the Spanda tradition of Kashmir Shaivism, the scholar Mark Dyczkowski writes, "Nothing is impure, all is perfect, including Māyā [the world of illusion] and the diversity it engenders."[7]

The eighteenth-century Christian theologian and philosopher Emanuel Swedenborg said that if our "internals" are open, we are in heaven right here and now. But this Christian approach to right view was expressed far earlier in esoteric Christianity with teachings like that from the Gnostic Gospel of Thomas, in which the disciples of Jesus ask him when the new world will come and Jesus replies, "What you look forward to has already come, but you do not recognize it." The disciples press again: "When will the Kingdom come?" And Jesus answers, "It will not come by waiting for it. It will not be a matter of saying, 'Here it is' or 'There it is.' Rather, the Kingdom of the Father is spread out upon the earth, and men do not see it."[8] The religious historian Elaine Pagels writes that, in such gospels, "This conviction—that whoever explores human experience simultaneously discovers divine reality—is one of the elements that marks Gnosticism as a distinctly religious movement. . . . *Allogenes* teaches that, first, one can come to know 'the good that is within.'"[9]

The Islamic tradition has much in common with the Christian narrative of basic goodness. The scholar Yūsuf al-Hurr explains in more detail: "Islam not only accepts the idea that we all have a fundamental celestial nature but also that its essence is *ramah* (compassion) and *nur* (light). Much of Islam focuses on stripping oneself of the layers of the false self to re-center our consciousness back to our true nature"—a return to alignment with divine order that is achieved through remembrance—"curing our spiritual amnesia."[10]

The principle of recollection, or remembering, is central in the Buddhist tradition and to meditation altogether. In fact, the Tibetan word for mindfulness, *drenpa*, means "to recollect." Distraction (to "draw apart"), is a form of contraction, and the opposite of "remembering." It involves a pulling apart from the present moment, which implies that mindlessness and forgetfulness are moment-to-moment expressions of our spiritual amnesia. The Tibetan teacher Lakar Rinpoche teaches that "to end distraction is to end samsāra." In essence, he is saying that when we conquer forgetfulness, teaching ourselves to come back to the present moment over and over—as we will be doing in the meditations that follow—we're also working with a deeper order of recollection: one that returns us not just to the present moment but eventually to our primordially pure nature.

Remember that contraction also means withdrawal, which has one of its most immediate expressions every single time we're dis-tracted from the present moment. So to end *contraction-distraction* is to end saṃsāra. Because this expression of contraction is so ubiquitous and accessible, we'll begin our formal meditations in part 2 with the user-friendly prac-tice of mindfulness. We'll then advance into the more refined healing practice of open awareness before finally venturing into the ultimate wholeness of the reverse meditations. Throughout this journey of heal-ing, you will discover, or remember, right view for yourself.

Even the word *religion* hints at this foundational return: *re-* ("back"), and *ligare* ("link")—to "link back" to wholeness—which also echoes our narrative of reversal. In other words, to remember is to reverse, to turn (*versus*) back (*re*). By turning back and going directly into that which we would normally flee (all our unwanted experiences), we will return to this foundational wholeness that is so quickly forgotten when things start to hurt.

The Vajra Regent, a modern teacher, said, "The essence of spiritual practice is remembrance." In our new language, the essence of spiritual practice is *reversal.* Speaking on behalf of the Vedantic tradition, the author Deepak Chopra was known for saying, "All this effort to learn, when all we have to do is remember." We are perfectly pure in nature. We just forgot. The purpose of the spiritual path is to jog your memory. In *Facets of Unity*, the spiritual teacher A. H. Almaas also emphasizes that the divine nature of the "real world" simply awaits our recognition:

> The intrinsic nature of everything is a loving, conscious quality, whether we're talking about physical objects, human beings, actions of a human being, or physical phenomena. . . . If we really see this, we are already in heaven. Wherever you turn, there is harmony, beauty, and love.[11]

Almaas suggests that no matter the outer qualities we observe in the world around us—and I would add, whether we experience things as painful or blissful—reality has an inner nature of lovingness, joyousness, and abundance that "transcends all appearances." With attention, "We see that all of existence is the manifestation of God, the Divine Being . . . it is perfect."[12]

Such recognition and attention are the essence of right view. Jewish mysticism, in the words of Zvi Ish-Shalom, offers words that are especially relevant to the path of reverse meditation:

> Do we trust that reality is inherently good and benevolent and will hold us as we move through the pain of our contractions? To have this kind of trust is not a small thing. The deeper in contraction we are, the more difficult it is to trust that it's okay to really sense into our contraction and embrace it and welcome it.[13]

"In the usual perspective we dislike contraction because it feels unholy and godless, and it hurts," says Ish-Shalom.

> But in this new view of wholeness, we accept the experience of contraction and the human experience of struggle with more appreciation for its Divine nature. With this appreciation comes a great curiosity about its significance, its meaning, and its purpose for us personally. There is an appreciation that there is something waiting, wanting to reveal itself to us. Rather than seeing contraction and its suffering as a problem to get rid of it, it is seen as an opportunity and a handout from God, as a gift to unwrap.[14]

BASICALLY GOOD PAIN

Although countless masters in numerous traditions have taught that even the most unwanted, painful, and challenging events should be viewed as basically good and perfectly pure, such a teaching often meets resistance and is rejected as just wrong: "You're trying to tell me that my heartbreak and pain are perfectly pure? Nonsense!" Reversing this kind of resistance is the mission of this book.

Ish-Shalom concludes, "It is through understanding our contractions that we unwrap these gifts"—of challenge, pain, and suffering. The book you are reading is intended to guide you toward the right view and the practices that bring it to life, to "unwrap these gifts," but also to unwrap all the wrong views in which the gifts have been packaged. Before we contract, which is what initiates the wrapping process, whatever arises is essentially pure. Chögyam Trungpa writes, "All phenomena are completely new and fresh, absolutely unique at the instant of their appearance and entirely free from all concepts of past, present, and future, as if experienced in another dimension of time."[15] What renders phenomena impure, therefore, is the stain of conceptuality (itself a form of contraction), which defiles what arises in the present with concepts from the past. "What kind of thing is direct reality before we have as yet added the complexities of thought?" asks the Japanese philosopher Nishida Kitaro in his book *A Study of Good.* "That is, what kind of thing is an event of pure experience? At this time there is not as yet the opposition of subject and object, there is not the separation into intellect, emotion, and will, there is only independent, self-contained, pure activity."[16]

So much of the spiritual path in general, and the journey of reverse meditation in particular, is one of negation—of negating, removing, unwrapping, or otherwise *reversing* all the wrong views and concepts to reveal what has been here all along.[17] Negation is the necessary stripping described by Yūsuf al-Hurr. We're going to open the gifts from God by removing all the hideous wrapping paper—the devilish obscurations, conceptions, and contractions—that cover it.

When it's finally revealed, right view is not the creation of a new view. Right view naturally discloses itself when all wrong views are erased. Right view is actually the only real view. Every other view is either partial or wrong. The Tibetan sage Milarepa sang, "The view is original wisdom which is empty." "Empty" here refers to how this original view of wisdom and goodness is empty of all confused views.

Our inability to recognize and abide by this truth of basic goodness and perfect purity is why we constantly try to manipulate our experience, and the world itself, into *our* version of perfect purity, our ideas about what is "good." The Austrian psychoanalyst Otto Rank believed that much of human suffering arises from our attempts to perfect the world. For several hundred years, the Inquisition burned countless people at the stake in an effort to purge Christianity of heretics. Hitler's "Final Solution" to the "Jewish problem" was his attempt to purify the earth of an entire population. Stalin, Pol Pot, and countless tyrants had their versions of perfection that created untold suffering.

Our own manipulations may be more personal and small-scale, but we still attempt to dictate experience—to clean it up into our versions of perfection—which just messes it up. These cleansing impulses transform simple pain into complex suffering. With the upcoming meditations, we can experience these misguided manipulations of reality every time we stub our toe.

THE TWO TRUTHS

To step into the lofty view of perfect purity, we need to understand the "two truths": absolute truth and relative truth. Otherwise, the trek up to this summit might be too precipitous, and right view is tossed into the dustbin of New Age rhetoric. How can we possibly reconcile a view that asserts the perfect purity of all phenomena with our knowledge about heartbreaks and horrors such as the Holocaust, genocide, birth defects, ecological devastation, and countless other undeniable truths? How does perfect purity explain human tragedy?

The view of perfect purity comes from the perspective of the ultimate or absolute truth, which is the unconditional and unconventional proclamation of *how things really are*. But the way we normally view things is from the perspective of relative or conditional truth—the conventional truth of *how things appear to be*. With right view, we're not denying appearance, but we are challenging the status of appearance. Our path in reverse meditation is to bring appearance into harmony with reality, as a way to alter our relationship to unwanted experience. What are things really like when you take a close look? What is pain, truly? What makes an unwanted experience unwanted? What's actually going on when we suffer?

In Buddhist language, relative truth applies to the world of form; absolute truth applies to the world of emptiness. We all know what form is because we live in the world of form, or appearances. Emptiness is not so obvious. Understanding emptiness, or *śūnyāta* in Sanskrit, requires a reversal of our conventional view of things and presents a challenge to the very idea of "thingness" itself. This includes things like pain, hardship, anxiety, fear, or any other unwanted experience. Understanding emptiness alters our relationship to some very practical things, and when brought to fruition, removes our suffering. Emptiness lies at the silent center of this book, so we need to start wrapping our mind around it.

First of all, *emptiness* does not mean "nothingness" or "nonexistence," nor a spooky kind of void. A friendlier translation would be "openness," "transparency," or "boundlessness." Emptiness refers to the absence of a falsely projected type of existence: the fallacious notion that things have inherent existence. *Emptiness* means "no-thingness." It means that if you take a very close look at anything, you will find that there is essentially no solid, lasting, and independent thing there. Things are empty of intrinsic existence, or self-nature. What you will find, if you take that close look, is a vast interconnected nexus of causes and conditions—a deep ecology, connecting everything to everything else.

Emptiness really means fullness. Being empty of "self" means being full of "other." So when we talk about a mending return to wholeness, we are talking about a return to emptiness-fullness. Emptiness teaches that the only "thing" that truly exists is relationship. Relationship to what? To other relationships. The Zen master Thich Nhat Hanh sums it up beautifully:

> If you are a poet, you will see clearly that there is a cloud floating in this sheet of paper. Without a cloud there will be no water; without water the trees cannot grow; and without trees, you cannot make paper. So the cloud is in here. The existence of this page is dependent on the existence of a

cloud. Paper and cloud are so close. Let us think of other things, like sunshine. Sunshine is very important because the forest cannot grow without sunshine, and we as humans cannot grow without sunshine. So the logger needs sunshine in order to cut the tree, and the tree needs sunshine in order to be a tree. Therefore, you can see sunshine in this sheet of paper. And if you look more deeply, with the eyes of a *bodhisattva*, with the eyes of those who are awake, you see not only the cloud and the sunshine in it, but that everything is here, the wheat that became the bread for the logger to eat, the logger's father—everything is in this sheet of paper. . . . This paper is empty of an independent self. Empty, in this sense, means that the paper is full of everything, the entire cosmos. The presence of this tiny sheet of paper proves the presence of the whole cosmos.[18]

Any systems-based, integral, or holistic approach to reality echoes the same tenets. Ecology, ecopsychology, general systems theory, chaos theory, and complexity theory are a few examples that render the principles of emptiness in modern terms. Quantum mechanics, the most successful theory in the history of science, makes similar proclamations. The physicist Carlo Rovelli describes quantum mechanics as "the discovery that the properties of any entity are nothing other than the way in which that entity influences others. It exists only through its interactions." He believes that "to understand nature, we must focus on these interactions rather than on isolated objects" and he emphasizes that "*there are no properties outside of interactions.*" Finally, he acknowledges, "This is a radical leap. It is equivalent to saying that everything consists *solely* of the way in which it affects something else."[19]

This understanding of nature, which includes a deeper understanding of the nature of pain and suffering, demands a reversal of our normal Aristotelian "thing-thinking," or Boolean black/white, true/false, yes/no binary logic. To understand emptiness demands that we discover the no-thingness nature of "things." What does this have to do with my pain and suffering, you ask? Everything.

The biggest reason we suffer is because we *reify*. To reify is to make things real, to transform a no-thing into a thing, to shrink-wrap relationships into objects, to freeze processes into products. To reify is to also imbue phenomena with power they intrinsically lack. Pain cannot inherently hurt you, unless you empower it by reifying it. And you reify it by contracting against it. Reification is the result of contraction. As we will see, reification is a relentless unconscious construction (contraction) project at the heart of all our hardship. To understand, and *practice*, the view of emptiness is to engage in a peaceful transfer of power back to its rightful source. Stripping the power that things appear to have, reversing it, and delivering it back home. It leads to the breathtaking discovery that emptiness cannot harm emptiness.

In our journey, we will analyze experiences like pain and suffering by separating them into their component parts. It's a "divide and conquer" approach, with a strong footing in science, that returns "things" to their empty nature and delivers power back to its original place. It's a reverse process of dereification. If contraction is the heart of reification, openness—that is, emptiness—is at the heart of dereification. The physicist Anthony Aguiree lends a hand in understanding this relationship between dereification and emptiness:

> We break things down into smaller and smaller pieces, but then the pieces, when examined, are not there. Just the arrangements of them are. What then, are *things*, like the boat, or its sails, or your fingernails? What *are* they? If things are forms of forms of forms of forms, and if forms are order, and order is defined by us . . . they exist, it would appear, only as created by, and *in relation to*, us and the Universe. They are, the Buddha might say, emptiness.[20]

For our purposes, emptiness refers to the fact that things like pain, suffering, and other unwanted experiences do indeed appear, but they're not essentially real. That's fantastically good news. It means you don't have to suffer the way you do. It means you can take responsibility for your own happiness and suffering, because you realize that both are of your own making. If you construct your suffering, you can deconstruct it. Instead of contracting, you can open. That's the reversal. We're going to demolish this thing called suffering, and return to the original construction site, to the ground zero of emptiness. But don't take my word for it. Test these teachings against your own experience. Do the upcoming meditations, and find out for yourself.

The view of emptiness, which is a more technical way of talking about basic goodness, is foreign to us. We're not familiar with it. We simply haven't experienced the world through the lens—or in this case non-lens—of emptiness and goodness. The Tibetan word for meditation is *gom*, which translates as "to become familiar with." This term has a number of implications, but here it refers to the journey of meditating upon, and becoming familiar with, this reverse view. By going into reverse, by opening instead of closing, we will finally see the world rightly.

WRONG VIEW

The view of emptiness and original purity goes against the grain of Western notions of reified things and original sin, which is the core *wrong view*. Basic goodness flies in the face of basic badness, and emptiness is the opposite of reification. The notion of original sin isn't even relative truth. It's just false. This wrong view leads to the feeling that reality is somehow deficient, that there's something missing, that we're not good enough. A foundational deficit disorder lurks within. So we consume to satisfy the hunger. The polymath Peter Kingsley writes,

> And there's a great secret: we all have that vast missingness deep inside us. The only difference between us and the mystics is that they learn to face what we find ways of running away from. That's the reason why mysticism has

been pushed to the periphery of our culture: because the more we feel that nothingness inside us, the more we feel the need to fill the void. . . . We've been taught in so many ways to escape from ourselves.[21]

This wrong view spawns all the pathologies of materialism, including its byproduct of consumerism, which never satisfies because we're eating the menu instead of the meal. We get lost in all manner of eateries, which results in all manner of obesities. Physical, intellectual, psychological, and even spiritual portliness (that is, spiritual materialism) starts right here. Bloated bellies and bookshelves, overstuffed attics and garages, overweight intellects and ideologies—the "obesity" epidemic, in its infinite forms, is creating a host of personal, collective, and environmental eating disorders that are devouring this planet.

Instead of getting full, we're just getting fat. Because we're just not getting it. We're doing the opposite of what needs to be done. Because we have the wrong view, we're looking in the wrong direction and consuming the wrong things. What we're really looking for—authentic consumption of experience—requires reversing our gaze and looking *within*. Now we're finally setting our sights on the proper target. The Greek word for "sin" is *hamartia*—"to miss the mark." If we have the wrong view, it's no surprise we continue to miss the mark. The true original sin is setting our sights in the wrong direction, which naturally gives rise to all the "wrongs" we see today.

Right view proclaims there is no deficiency, no lack, nothing whatsoever missing "out there." *We're* the ones who have gone AWOL on reality. What we're looking for, what we really want, we already have, even when what we have is painful. We just have to set our gaze in the right direction, and there it is. *Here* it is—hiding in plain sight.

To reverse the "obesity" epidemic in all its forms, we need a strict diet of truth. False consumerism is then transformed into genuine consumerism, and the liberating realization that what we really want to devour is experience itself—no matter how nasty or nice. Joseph Campbell said:

People say that what we're all seeking is a meaning for life. I don't think that's what we're really seeking. I think that what we're seeking is an experience of being alive, so that our life experiences on the purely physical plane will have resonances within our innermost being and reality, so that we actually feel the rapture of being alive.[22]

Right consumerism, born from right view, is about the ecstasy of being fully alive, an ecstasy that we will paradoxically discover by going fearlessly into our agony.

CHAPTER 2

DISCOVERING THE SACRED
IN THE PROFANE

Kedumah ultimately holds a radically inclusive view
in which everything is recognized to be a sacred part
of the ultimately unified whole, including the most
mundane, ordinary, and even disturbing experiences of
contraction. . . . With a bit of guidance and practice, it is
totally possible for our suffering to transform into freedom.

—ZVI ISH-SHALOM

In *Ethics for a Small Planet*, the American theologian Daniel Maguire
calls for revising our ideas about the distinction between the sacred
and the profane, suggesting that "to project the experience of the
sacred onto an immaterial God is to shortchange sacredness as a
dimension of material life and turn it into an object of worship that
is beyond our world and thus alien to life."[1] However, proclaiming
that reality is sacred by nature is usually not enough to convert us to
the right view. To embrace this sanctified vision requires expanding
our notions of goodness, perfection, and divinity—a mental shift that
immediately alters our understanding of badness, imperfection, and
the profane. The ancient bodies of knowledge collectively known as the

wisdom traditions, and the meditations that support them, invite us to discover for ourselves that if we just leave things alone (and leaving things alone properly is the art of meditation), there is absolutely nothing whatsoever missing—even when life is difficult. As Trungpa Rinpoche often said, "There is no such thing as an underdeveloped moment." Ego—a word I'll be using simply to mean "the sense of self"—as the grand developer, may want to improve upon any given moment, but in doing so it ironically plunders it.

The Great Perfection (Dzogchen) tradition is often translated as "Great Completion," which alludes to the fact that every moment, no matter how difficult, is still complete. Because of our wrong views, *we* are the ones who stain reality with our versions of how it should be, thereby rendering it incomplete. We are the ones who project our hopes, fears, ideologies, beliefs, and expectations onto reality, corrupting it in our image. We are the ones who impute a sense of deficiency onto a world that is essentially abundant. An impoverished view of reality is the result of *our* poverty mentality, an internal deficit disorder that we project onto the bountiful world. The Christian mystic Meister Eckhart said, "The moment you get ideas, God fades out and the Godhead too. It is when the idea is gone that God gets in. . . . If you are to know God divinely, your own knowledge must become as pure ignorance, in which you forget yourself and every other creature."[2]

Sacred outlook has a unique role in this book. On one hand, it is the ideal *prerequisite* view that allows us to trust the reverse meditations. If we know in our bones that even the most unwanted experiences are essentially sacred, we'll be willing to go directly into those difficult states because we'll understand we have nothing to fear—and everything to look forward to.[3] Freedom is to be found by going directly into unwanted experiences, not by continually running away from them. Nothing can imprison us if we realize the walls are of our own making. Sacred outlook is the "reverse view" that allows us to overturn our relationship to hardship and to boldly go where we have never gone before.

On the other hand, sacred outlook is also the *result* of the reverse meditations. By going deeply into our contractions and unwanted experiences, and transforming our relationships to them, we discover the purity hidden within the profanity. With the right view, we will say to ourselves, "I never knew that so much light was hidden in all this darkness!" "There's so much energy and life in here!" "I had no idea such freedom existed in all this contraction!" Trungpa Rinpoche writes:

> The everyday practice is simply to develop a complete acceptance and openness to all situations and emotions and to all people, experiencing everything totally without mental reservations and blockages, so that one never withdraws [contracts] or centralizes onto oneself. This produces a tremendous energy which is usually locked up in the processes of mental evasion and generally running away from life experiences. Clarity of awareness may in its initial stages be unpleasant or fear inspiring. If so, then one should open oneself completely to the pain or the fear and welcome it.[4]

So the Dzogchen view of perfect purity is a "fake it till you make it" view. It's not easy at first to see the world as pure, let alone see the purity of all the unwanted experiences that arise within it. On a relative and unexamined level, life is really hard. But that's only because we haven't examined it properly.

Socrates said, "The unexamined life is not worth living," and he dared to challenge the prevailing wrong views of his day. His attempts at reversing them cost him his life. Challenging the wrong views of our day will not cost you your life, but it will cost you your ego—because ego is the limited bandwidth of your identity that perceives things wrongly. Ego is the part of you that only wants to feel good, that is born from contraction itself and shrinks away from anything that feels bad. By reversing your relationship to unwanted experience, you're simultaneously transcending the ego, which is nothing more than an arrested form of development. Ego falls away as you release the contractions that create it.

On an absolute and examined level, life is celebratory and divine. It becomes tortuous only when you don't know how to find the goodness.

By the end of this book, you will see for yourself that your greatest fears are basically good, your heartbreak is perfectly pure, your pain and suffering are inviolate—if you don't violate them with your improper relationship. But for now, I'm asking you to simply trust the wisdom traditions that proclaim the radical truth of basic goodness. Have faith in those who speak from direct experience. In the next chapters we'll follow in their footsteps and test their findings. Meanwhile, imagine how life would change if you discovered this truth for yourself. (Spoiler: You would discover not liberation *from* the world, but *into* it.)

THE SECULAR VIEW

Because we're brought up in a world that presumes the primacy of matter, a materialistic worldview, we take that view as axiomatic, a given. This view proclaims that everything comes from matter, and is therefore reducible to it. We tend to also assume that the secular worldview is a neutral assessment, an accurate baseline understanding of "what the world really is" that is then colored by spiritual or religious ideology. "But secularity is not simply the everyday world we actually dwell in," writes the philosopher David Loy. "It is a historically conditioned understanding of where and what we are." He continues:

> The secular world that we now understand ourselves to be living in was originally one half of a duality, and it remains haunted by the loss of its other half. Modernity developed out of a split that developed between God's transcendence and a de-spiritualized material world. Until the modern era, God was believed to be the source of meaning and value, so when God eventually disappeared up into the clouds, we were left to cope as best we could in what was left: a desacralized mechanistic universe.[5]

The secular worldview, which can be seen as a subset of materialism, is therefore a mere interpretation of reality, not the baseline or true reality.

How do we know that a sacred outlook is the right view? Can we be sure it's not just another interpretation? Outside of scriptural authority, and the experiential validity of tuning in to a sacred world (it feels like coming home), look at the results of the desacralized view. The world is going to hell ecologically, politically, socially, and economically because we've lost sight of the right view. Our standard view is not in harmony with reality, and that raging dissonance is evident everywhere we turn. How much louder does it have to get before we wake up to the inconvenient truth that our materialistic view is out of tune? Loy writes:

> What may be misleading about this discussion of an enervated sacral dimension is that it still seems to suggest superimposing something (for example, some particular religious understanding of the meaning of our lives) onto the secular world (that is, the world "as it really is"). My point is the opposite [reverse]: our usual understanding of the secular is a deficient worldview (in Buddhist terms, a delusion) distorted by the fact that one half of the original duality has gone missing, although now it has been absent so long that we have largely forgotten about it.[6]

In chapter 1 we looked at how remembrance can be viewed as the essence of spiritual practice. In this chapter, we'll see how this includes remembering sacred view—especially when we're in pain.

OPENING TO THE SACRED

Because the sacred worldview is so antithetical to our secular ways, we can further open the door to seeing the profound in the profane by examining our relationship to traditional sacred spaces. What is it that generates the experience of the sacred in conventional ways? Is it evoked by something external, like having your breath taken away upon entering the majesty of St. Peter's Cathedral in Rome? Or is it an inner receptivity that opens you to the sacred? Or some combination of both? The former is a more relative and conditional evocation, arising from something outside; the latter is more absolute and unconditional, arising from within. Our journey is to tap into the unconditional, which allows us to discover heaven even when we hurt. But we can use conditional expressions to help us actualize the unconditional.

In his influential book *The Sacred and the Profane*, the religious scholar Mircea Eliade explores the ingredients of religious experience by examining the term *heirophany*—"the manifestation of the sacred." This comes from the Greek *heiros* ("sacred, holy") and *phainein* ("to bring to light, to reveal"). When we elevate our relationship to phenomena, we discover the sacred in the profane. And a higher relationship is something we can cultivate. Eliade writes, "For those who have a religious experience all nature is capable of revealing itself as cosmic sacrality. The cosmos in its entirety can become a heirophany."[7]

The experience of heirophany is equally an epiphany when the sacred is revealed in the most unwanted experiences. With the right view, even pain becomes a sacrament, "that is, a communion with the sacred."[8] It's absolutely eye-popping when we unwrap the gifts from God packaged in the ugliest wrapping paper, and discover the sacred in what we previously deemed sacrilegious.

Because of the massive influence of science and secularity, Western views are largely profane. Science attempts to reduce everything into the building blocks of matter, and in so doing it degrades the life and light out of things. It's an "endarkened" view, far removed from the enlightened outlook. In the wry words of the philosopher Ken Wilber, everything we perceive, including all life forms, is just the complex play of frisky dirt. A similar shrink-wrapping occurs with the Western view of original sin, a view as degraded as scientific reductionism. The triple-barreled force of science, secularity, and Western religion demotes reality.

Our intention in this book is to replace reductionism with elevationism, demotion with promotion, and degrading with upgrading. Instead of reducing everything to impure matter, we will elevate everything into pure spirit. "Pure spirit" is a feeble way to depict the ineffable. The Japanese word *kokoro*, "heart-mind-spirit," comes closer, but no finite word can embrace the infinite. And although we may use the word *elevationism* to refer to the reverse of the reductionist view, this new view is elevated only because it stands in sharp contrast to our tainted views. In essence, "elevation" to the sacred view is actually very ordinary. It's the natural state. Reducing everything into the profanity of lifeless matter is what's unnatural. So the sacred world appears elevated only from our sullied reductionist stance.

SACRED SPACE

Perception is always generated in contrast. We see these dark letters because they're set against the background of a white page. Similarly, we can learn about what is sacred by comparing it to what it is not. The traditional understanding of the sacred is that it represents something set apart from the secular, apart from the profane. We often set off sacred space by means of thresholds, boundaries, and perimeters in order to exclude the profane. We might physically enclose a space by building a temple, cathedral, or shrine that serves as a material protector to keep the sacrilegious out.

Eliade writes about how the threshold to the sacred is often guarded by fierce protectors, stationed at the entryways to keep evil spirits out: "The threshold has its guardians—gods and spirits who forbid entrance both to human enemies and to demons and powers of pestilence."[9] In my spiritual practice, I often participate as part of a group in a sādhanā (involving elaborate liturgical rituals) that begins with a "setting of the boundaries" that serves a function like the one Eliade describes. Protectors are placed at the gates of the sacred mandala that is about to be created. In these practices, we recite wrathful mantras, play percussive instruments, assume aggressive mudras ("gestures"), offer tormas ("sacrificial cakes"), walk the perimeter of the room with purifying smoke to exorcise demonic energies, and throw mustard seeds to evict any evil spirits that could despoil the mandala. While the rituals are external, the demons being exorcised are mostly internal: "the powers of pestilence" that constitute our wrong views and degraded concepts. We don't have to add anything (but right view) to perceive the world as sacred. We only need to keep the wrong views out, and the world reveals its divinity.

When we enter a sacred space, we're moved; we're touched; we feel something different. In this regard, the sacred and the aesthetic become intimately connected. The sacred *is* aesthetic in the way it wakes us up and brings us to our senses, making us more fully present. Our senses operate only in the present moment—we can't literally see the past or hear the future. So in coming to our senses, we come to nowness. We enter reality, which only takes place in the present moment.

The physical frames that we use to evoke a sense of the sacred can be compared to the way we use frames to designate art. In both cases, frames serve to heighten aesthetic impact by successively concentrating, and therefore consecrating, our awareness. Art in a museum is framed by the museum itself, and then secondarily by the frame around the artwork. And both art and the sacred are evoked not only by what is inside the frame but also by what is kept out. David Loy writes that the frames we put around art (like the frames we put around the sacred) serve as protection "from our usual utilitarian preoccupations"; the frames are a means of "keeping certain ways of thinking *out* of them."[10]

The sacred is a portal to reality. As Eliade says, "the sacred is preeminently the *real*."[11] In its fundamental realness, the sacred is simultaneously a magical experience and a very ordinary one—so ordinary it becomes extraordinary. In fact, in Tibetan Buddhism, the mind that experiences enlightenment—what we could refer to as ultimate sacredness—is called "ordinary mind" (*thamal gyi shepa*). It's called "ordinary" because it's the foundational mind, a simple mind free of heady elaboration or embellishment—our purest mind before it's stained by the impurities of conceptual proliferation. Simply put, the unearthing of that ordinary mind *is* enlightenment.

This connection to the ordinary is another instance of reversal. We tend to imagine enlightenment as something truly ecstatic—fireworks that never end or some mind-blowing extravaganza. But it's the total inverse of that. It's fantastically ordinary, so ordinary that we constantly miss it. We're looking for a Hollywood-level experience when it's more like Kansas (I love Kansas). So we rush past it on our way to grander productions. As we'll see later in this book, the initial glimpse of enlightenment can be orgasmic, a cosmic release of epic proportions. But that's only because of the intensity of the preceding contraction.

In other words, if we're really contracted, the initial opening can be dramatic. But if we're already open, the experience of enlightenment is utterly ordinary. As the Zen master Suzuki Roshi said, "Enlightenment was my biggest disappointment." Indeed, from ego's (wrong) point of view, enlightenment is the ultimate letdown.

If the sacred is aesthetic, waking us up to reality, the profane is anesthetic. It puts us to sleep; it deadens us to reality, in the spiritual sense. We experience the profane—we *generate* the non-sense of the profane—whenever we lose contact with our senses and get pulled into distraction. To dis-tract is to "draw apart." Distraction is therefore a subtle form of anesthesia, a way we try to shield ourselves from the intensity of the moment. Especially when we're dealing with unwanted experiences, we attempt to anesthetize ourselves by leaping out of our sensory body and into our insensate head. In the upcoming meditations, we'll reverse that trajectory and descend back into the wisdom of our sensual body.

Saying that the sacred is a gateway to reality is another way of saying that it's a portico into the present moment, since the present moment is the only possible reality, the only thing that *is*. The Zen author Vanessa Zuisei Goddard writes: "In sacred places it's easier for us to see the *is*ness or suchness of a place or a thing, which in turn leads to a basic kind of regard: the valuing of something simply because it *is*. Sacred space thus reveals even the most ordinary things as they truly are: *holy*, from the root of the word *whole*."[12]

The holy as the experience of the whole (the Great Completion, or Dzogchen) means that when we're fully present, when our attention and presence are whole, we realize the sacredness that is always already present. The implication is that we don't have to wait to enter a sacred space to be touched by the divine. The body itself can be a temple, and *the sacred is something we can actually practice within ourselves.* By creating the proper space inside of us, we behold the sacred outside.

We enter the essence of St. Peter's Cathedral when we're fully present to what's happening, even if that happening is hurting.

SACRED TIME

The sacred can be created not merely through an elevated relationship to space but also through a more refined relationship to time. Rabbi Abraham Joshua Heschel viewed the Sabbath as "a sanctuary which we build, *a sanctuary in time*." In the same way that a cathedral, mosque, shrine, or other place of worship can serve as a physical frame that demarcates a sacred space, temporal frames such as Christmas, Ramadan, Rosh Hashanah, or Losar can serve as temples in time. Briefer rites, such as Communion during Mass on Christmas or the moment of transmission in a Kalachakra empowerment, offer temporal frameworks that charge a moment in time, rendering it sacred.

For one day a week (Sabbath) or one month a year (Ramadan), for instance, members of some religions sanctify time by choosing to relate to it differently. They are invited to be more present, mindful, and aware, which blesses their experience of that day or month. The perception of the sacred is therefore attitudinal—and more specifically, attentional. But any of us can change our attitudes and discover the Sabbath in every second. We can refine our attention with meditation, and make every day a holy day.

The profane moment, by contrast, is a distracted moment. Profanity occurs when the mind is flitting back and forth between the past and the future, pillaging the present by diluting it. When the present moment is held with complete mindfulness, presence itself becomes the cathedral. In the spirit of the Great Completion, or Great Wholeness, when we do the laundry or wash the dishes with complete presence, that becomes as sacred as walking into St. Peter's.

THE SACRED POINT

These sanctifying principles are of paramount importance when it comes to working with pain and the reverse meditations, because our default relationship to any unwanted experience is to dilute it by getting away from it. When we hurt, we want out. The default move is to anesthetize, to dis-tract from the ferocity of the experience—which, ironically, transforms pain into suffering. We inject anesthetic by ejecting from the pain, evicting awareness from our sensual bodies into our insensate heads.[13] If the pain itself is coming from the mind, as when we grieve, worry, or catastrophize, we try to escape through countless other forms of "distraction therapy," like substance abuse, entertainment, or the diversion of relentless activity.

Does anyone in their right mind want to stay present with their pain, to be *fully* in pain? In fact, yes: spiritual warriors. Those wearing the armor of right view. When a spiritual warrior hurts, they go *into* the conflict. Protected with the right view, they fearlessly march into battle, not to defeat the pain they're feeling, but to enter it fully, to befriend it, and therefore transform it.

In Islam, this transformation is the goal of greater jihad, the deepest type of "holy war"—which means doing the difficult inner work, battling the karmic or habitual forces within, in order to discover the wholeness (holiness) of whatever arises.[14] Waging a real holy war is being willing to sacrifice yourself, your ego, your wrong views, your identity—anything that separates you from painful realities. This sacrifice is for the greater good, which is basic goodness, or wholeness itself. His Holiness the Dalai Lama is such a warrior. His Tibetan name is Kunden, which means "presence"—or in our context, wholeness. In one of the central quotes for our journey, Trungpa Rinpoche writes:

> We could say that the real world is that in which we experience pleasure and pain, good and bad. . . . *But if we are completely in touch with these dualistic feelings, that absolute experience of duality is itself the experience of non-duality.* Then there is no problem at all, because duality is seen from a

perfectly open and clear point of view in which there is no conflict; there is a tremendous encompassing vision of oneness. Conflict arises because duality is not seen as it is at all. It is only seen in a biased way, a very clumsy way. In fact, [because of our wrong views] we do not perceive anything properly. . . . So when we talk about the dualistic world as confusion, that confusion is not the complete dualistic world, but only half-hearted.[15]

When things hurt, we don't want to be completely in touch with our pain. We want to be literally out of touch. We don't want to feel anything. So we contract away from our pain to anesthetize ourselves, and these contractions give birth to duality, the ultimate profanity. If we have the courage to reverse our normal strategy, and go fully into our dualistic feelings, duality transforms into nonduality. It's our half-hearted relationship to pain that's the problem, not pain itself. A whole-hearted relationship reveals pain to be sacred. Right view, conjoined with the meditations that bring it to life, provides this new relationship.

CHAPTER 3

THE VIEW BEHIND THE MEDITATIONS

The gift of learning to meditate is the greatest
gift you can give to yourself in this lifetime.

—LAKAR RINPOCHE

Once I discovered that I could enter heaven by embracing
hell, embracing hell became a core practice.

—CHRISTOPHER M. BACHE

To ease our way into a proper relationship to unwanted experience,
the formal meditations in part 2 of this book will begin with entry-
level exercises. We're going to slowly stretch our mind into expansive
positions, like mental yoga, that allow us to contain increasingly difficult life experiences. Stretching might not always feel good, but it's
good for growth.

Part 2 will begin with mindfulness—or more specifically, referential
meditation: that is, shamatha. *Shamatha* means "peace" or "tranquility,"
and the referential aspect in chapter 7 becomes important in chapter 8
when we transition into the practice of open awareness, or nonreferential

meditation. These qualifiers help us understand the evolution of one practice to the next. Briefly, *referential* means referring the mind back to some hitching post in meditation—be it your body, breath, a mantra, or a candle—whenever you stray into distraction. "Nonreferential" relates to the removal of that hitching post, and learning how to rest in awareness itself. We'll expand on all this in subsequent chapters.

The initial practice of mindfulness is mandatory because it provides the stability upon which we build the more advanced meditations. Without it, every other practice is on shaky ground. Each practice in part 2 follows the theme of "transcend and include," which means that as we go beyond mindfulness into the practice of open awareness, and then further into the reverse meditations, we never leave mindfulness (or open awareness) behind. Paradoxically, as we transcend mindfulness through these more advanced meditations, we'll strengthen our mindfulness and appreciate it even more.

As brilliant as the practices of mindfulness and open awareness are, they have limits. One limitation is that both of these meditations are nurtured in a peaceful and controlled environment, and we don't live in a peaceful and controlled world. If we practice meditation only while sitting in silence, for example, we tend to lose our meditative mind when we move, or when things get rowdy. With a sequestered and limited view of meditation, our practice becomes too precious and fragile. When we first start to practice, the meditative mind is a neonate, and an incubator helps. But we can't live our lives in an incubator. At a certain point we need to step out in order to grow up. If we don't, meditation itself can slip into an insidious form of distraction, pulling us away from raucous reality. Our charter is to eventually cultivate industrial strength meditation; we are nurturing a mind that can handle anything.

If we're not careful, meditation easily slips into a form of escape, and the meditative path turns into just another version of our comfort plan. There's nothing fundamentally wrong with taking refuge in the silence and stillness of sitting meditation or with being comfortable when we meditate. If we only associate the meditative mind with silence, stillness, and comfort, we're missing the point of authentic spiritual practice.

When Joseph Campbell proclaimed, "Follow your bliss," he was uttering a partial truth. But if we only follow our bliss, we'll just get blissed out. What happens to your bliss when you enter blistering life experiences? Are you able to find your bliss in an emotional blast furnace?

We'll return to a complete explanation of mindfulness, open awareness, and the reverse meditations after we further stabilize the right view.

BEFRIENDING CONTRACTION

The meditations in this book are intended to help you develop a nuanced relationship to contraction in its myriad forms. As a general rule, the further and deeper we go, the more potent and chronic the contraction. And the level of contraction is directly proportional to the discomfort it seeks to avoid. In other words, the deeper we go, the more challenging it gets. The deepest contractions have been with us a long time. They are not easily accessed, nor readily released. We've invested so much in them. To reach and relax these foundational cramps is to challenge our sense of reality, and our very sense of self. At these deepest levels, we contract as if our lives depend on it.

We're going to challenge the very axioms of life—the things that we take for granted—and point out that they are not givens but are merely constant constructions born from these constant contractions. These alleged truisms (that my pain is real; that I really exist; that the world is solid, lasting, and independent; that you are separate from me; that duality is real) are actually false. That unsettling exposure is like having a series of rugs pulled out from under us, and it can elicit the very reactions we're trying to avoid. In other words, what we'll explore can appear so groundless, and represents such a reversal of conventional views, that it might elicit contractions in the form of resistance, skepticism, or outright dismissal. These contractions unconsciously reestablish the sense of familiar ground. This is where it helps to remember the definition of meditation (*gom*): "to become familiar with." It takes time to become familiar with new ground, with material that is so foreign and antithetical to our normal ways.

If we relate to the rug pulling properly, the result is freedom, and eventually enlightenment. But if we don't, the open space that is invited is experienced as a free fall, and we panic. This panic is revelatory, for it shows us precisely why we contract in the first place. Contraction is ultimately a form of self-defense. It actually generates the very sense of self and is foundational in the construction of our dualistic world.

But the good news is that the energy that's been trapped in these contractions is directly proportional to the depth and duration of the contraction. This means that atomic energy is waiting to be accessed and released, which will energize your life beyond your wildest dreams. And once the contractions have been released, the energy that flows through you is completely renewable.

Imagine that every muscle in your body seizes up. Think of all the energy that is trapped in this nightmarish scenario. Now imagine that this total-body cramp has been going on for so long that you've adapted to it. Yes, life is hard, you're stiff as a board, but you endure it. Even though you've learned to live with it, all this energy is being used to sustain these cramps. Now imagine how it would feel if this seizure were released. Vast stores of energy would be unleashed, and you would feel like you'd come to life for the very first time. The experience would be liberating and ecstatic—well worth any effort needed to attain it.

Armed with the tools in this book, the deeper you go, and the more you relax the primordial cramps, the more liberating the journey becomes. To reach these deepest cramps, you have to gradually work your way down from the outermost levels to the thermonuclear core.

CONSTANCY

The first challenge in exploring contraction (as discussed in chapter 1) is the inevitable discomfort of the journey. The second challenge, which we return to here and in the next three chapters, is working with the subtle, ubiquitous, and unconscious dimensions of contraction. By focusing our beginning meditations on more conscious and overt contractions, we can literally get a feel for them. Once we're sensitized to their presence, we'll discover that contractions are everywhere. We're contracting all the time, and at so many levels. We'll also discover how desensitized we've become to the deeper levels of contraction—a form of anesthesia that manifests as literal insensitivity and insensibility. So another general rule is that the deeper you go, the more constant and unconscious is the cramp.

The constancy is what makes the deeper contractions more difficult to identify and discharge. It's like the proverbial fish unable to identify the environment in which it swims. Until it leaps out of the water, the fish has no contrast to detect its liquid environment. No contrast, no perception. Sometimes the onset of the contraction occurs so slowly it goes undetected. The result is what the ethnobotanist Terence McKenna calls "lethal cultural adaptation." You adapt to the cramp, and no longer see it as such. The contraction transforms into the baseline of your being, into "just the way it is."

Some of the following meditations therefore serve to create new contrast mediums that allow us to take that liberating leap, and to then see or feel things never seen or felt before. For example, in our first practice, when we sit still in mindfulness meditation (referential shamatha, in chapter 7), that stasis facilitates the perception of the movement of mind, or mental content. The relentless flow of thoughts is usually masked by the relentless activities of our lives. When we stop and sit, we're removing the camouflage of movement, and our thoughts now stand out. This phenomenon is why beginning meditators often complain that meditation is making things worse: "I never had so many thoughts before!" Yes, you did; you just never saw them. You've simply adapted to their persistent onslaught (an individual manifestation of lethal cultural adaptation).

Our second practice, of open awareness (in chapter 8), serves a similar function, creating a second contrast medium. By inviting the mind to open and expand, you can better see how it tends to close and contract. Now, it's not just the discovery that "I never realized how many thoughts I have!" but also "I never realized how contracted I am!" Both discoveries can be prickly, making things initially seem worse. It's like when I did yoga for the first time: I had no idea I was so stiff. But like a doctor making a diagnosis, the uncomfortable revelations are fundamentally curative. You can't solve a problem you don't even know you have.

ALWAYS PRACTICING, ALWAYS CONTRACTING

Meditation allows us to become familiar with who we are. By providing successive contrast mediums, meditation permits us to see dimensions of our being never seen before. It brings unconscious processes into the light of awareness, which allows us to liberate ourselves from them. Most of our contractions are automatic and unconscious reactions to unwanted experiences. We're automatons, running on automatic ignorance, habitually contracting with no idea that we're doing so. In the following pages, we'll unearth layer upon layer of these reflexive contractions.

Whether we know it or not, we're *always* meditating. We're always becoming increasingly familiar with whatever we experience, or whatever is our default. This means that we're always meditating on either contraction in its many guises, or openness in its numerous manifestations. One reason contraction is such a central player is because we're always practicing it, and therefore becoming increasingly familiar with it. We're too familiar with it, which again ironically masks it. We don't see it as a practice anymore. Contraction, reactivity, tension, withdrawal, and countless other iterations we'll explore have become a constant performance. We've accomplished the practice of contraction.

When I did my three-year retreat, I was introduced to dozens of practices. I took it upon myself to probe each practice deeply and to ask challenging questions of the meditation masters who introduced them to me. I wanted to understand what I was doing and why. One question I always asked was, "What does it mean to accomplish this practice?" How do you know when you're done practicing? One sign that I learned is that you start doing the practice automatically. The practice starts to "do you." Your default setting changes. You start to live the practice.

For example, even though I've practiced mindfulness for years, I'm still not mindful all the time. I am less distracted than before, but I still slip into mindlessness. I've cut such a deep groove with so many years of mindlessness that this fault, my default, will take time to fill in. I have not accomplished mindfulness, so I continue to practice it.

When we fall into our habitual patterns, and end up doing things we later regret, we often say something like "I just couldn't help myself." Because many of us unknowingly practice selfishness all the time, we tend to default into selfish behavior. Reversing this lifelong selfish practice with selflessness takes time. We know we're starting to accomplish selflessness when *that* becomes our default, and we say things like "I just couldn't help being selfless. I couldn't help but be generous, kind, and caring." Most genuine selflessness doesn't come with this kind of auto-commentary, but you get the point.

We've been practicing contraction for a very long time, pinching ourselves from time immemorial. It's our default. This isn't meant to discourage us as we start to counteract this lifelong habit but to point out how formidable it remains. Appreciating the sophistication, omnipresence, and power of contraction will help us marvel at it and gradually relax it.

OBSTACLE INTO OPPORTUNITY

A more playful approach also helps us unwind our tension more effectively than would an adversarial approach. Wrestling with our contractions only makes the cramp worse. We can learn to smile at contraction, make friends with it, and eventually use it as one of the most powerful indicators for precisely where we need to go to grow. In other words, armed with the right view, and with our heightened sensitivity, we can bring contraction onto the path and use it to *accelerate* our awakening. As Zvi Ish-Shalom says, "Any experience of contraction can be a portal to deeper states of Being and expansion."[1]

If we continue to capitulate to the force of our contractive habits, we'll continue to practice samsāra. But if we use those same contractions as an invitation to open instead of close, to expand instead of contract, our unconscious practice of samsāra transforms into the conscious practice of nirvāṇa. The tantric traditions of the East transform poison into medicine, and the alchemical traditions of the West transform lead into gold. With the right view, and the right meditations, we transform obstacle into opportunity and use every instance of contraction as an occasion to wake up. The curse transforms into a blessing.

SHORT AND SWEET

Our path of reverse meditation will include traditional longer meditations, as well as brief practices that can be used on the spot. The formal practices stabilize the mind, but the short practices help to bring meditation into life. In the highest schools of Tibetan Buddhism, "short sessions repeated often" are the main form of practice.

In Buddhist practice, a "near enemy" is the shadow side of a luminous quality. For example, the near enemy of compassion is pity, and the near enemy of confidence is hubris. One near enemy of formal sessions is that meditators often leave their meditative mind behind when they step into the world. The point of practice altogether is to mix meditation with post-meditation—to bring your meditative mind to everything. Many of the following meditations are designed for immediate use in life, which is akin to putting your meditation cushion in your back pocket. Meditations as short as one breath, or even a flash of openness, expand the meditative mind into life. Like drops of water adding up to fill a pool, these drops of meditation add up to saturate your life. The brevity doesn't lessen the profundity.

CHAPTER 4

THE FORCEFUL SUPER CONTRACTORS

Pain is inevitable; suffering is optional.

—THE DALAI LAMA

According to Hindu mythology, the world is supported by a great elephant, which is in turn supported by a great tortoise. When someone asked a Hindu sage what the great tortoise rests upon, the sage replied, "Another turtle." And what supports that turtle? "Ah, Sahib," remarked the sage, "after that it's turtles all the way down." And so it is with contraction. Contraction is the great elephant in the room, and once we become aware of its omnipresence, we realize it is contractions all the way down.

Contractions manifest along a spectrum, from temporary to constant, acute to chronic, covert to overt, and conscious to unconscious. Contractions are individual as well as collective, microcosmic and macrocosmic, literal and metaphorical, epistemological and ontological, and cognitive and somatic. They're behind everything, including our sense of "thingness" altogether. And they're certainly behind our pain.

Because contraction is a cosmic principle, it first manifests at spiritual levels, then crystallizes into psychological, mental, emotional, and eventually physical levels. These gradations are degrees of energetic constrictions. For example, psycho-spiritual levels include contraction manifesting as our very sense of self. Mental levels occur every time we identify with a thought or grasp after mental content. Whenever we objectify or reify anything, we're contracting. Emotional levels manifest from highly contractive states like anger and fear, to mid-level contractions like pride, jealousy, or passion, to refined levels that even include feelings like empathy and compassion. Physical levels include layers of tension all the way down to the cellular level.

Once we're sensitized to the ways we pinch, bind, squeeze, withdraw, confine, constrict, condense, tighten, reduce, narrow, withdraw, isolate, diminish, cut off, shrink, and otherwise close down, we'll start to see contraction everywhere. But just seeing it won't transform us. We need to *feel* how insanely contracted we are. Transformation takes place once we feel things. Our journey will allow us to feel how we contract and to use this feeling as an opportunity to open. The ubiquitous nature of contractions then turns in our favor. What previously obstructed our path now accelerates it.

We have to acknowledge both the healthy and unhealthy aspects of contraction, otherwise we'll start to contract against our contractions. Not all manifestations are negative. Without the positive expressions of contraction, we couldn't live or operate in the world. On a biological level, our heart contracts before it expands. Inhalation is the result of diaphragmatic contraction. Physical motion is the result of muscle contraction. Contracting away from fire prevents a painful burn. Our pupils contract to shield the retina from too much light. The philosopher and computer scientist Bernardo Kastrup says:

> There is a basic level of contraction that is just our natural inheritance. We shouldn't beat ourselves over the head because of that level of contraction, because that's what characterizes the human condition. We evolved to be psychologically invested to a basic level of contraction. The problem is that we've made it a lot worse because of culture . . . which has led us to take ourselves way too bloody seriously.[1]

On an individual and social level, contraction creates secure boundaries and generates defensive strategies necessary for survival. We need to withdraw from dangerous situations and isolate from harmful environments. Healthy contraction also includes the ability to focus and concentrate. Saying "no" in appropriate circumstances prevents manipulation, asserts proper authority, is a beneficial expression of limitation, and remains the heart of discipline. Meditative forms of contraction—gathering and collecting the mind—result in samādhi ("absorption states") and sampten ("steady mind"). Examples of wholesome contraction, at physical, psychological, and spiritual levels, are legion.

WHY THE SQUEEZE?

On a philosophical and spiritual level, the basic reason we contract in so many unwholesome ways is because as sentient beings we live in a contracted dimension of consciousness. Let me take you on a brief tour of spiritual cosmology, to help you understand the origins of your contracted experience as a human being, so you can appreciate why almost everything you do recapitulates this contractive narrative. (And meanwhile, keep in mind that all these preparatory comments are designed to support the outrageous reverse meditations. Without this backing, you won't do them.)

The wisdom traditions describe three general states of consciousness: waking, dreaming, and dreamless sleep. Western philosophy derives its views of mind and reality exclusively from the waking state, while Eastern schools—more inclusive, integral, and therefore complete—draw their views from all three states. In the context of reverse meditation, our view of relating to pain and hardship is Eastern in spirit, embracing the entire spectrum of consciousness—more open-minded in scope than its contracted Western counterpart.

Deep, dreamless sleep, sometimes referred to as *causal consciousness*, is the most open (and "empty," or śūnyā) of the three states. It's the irreducible state from which the other two crystallize, hence the term "causal." It also reveals the truest dimension of our being, and of reality itself.[2] This understanding of dreamless sleep is the *reverse* of Western views, which assert that the waking state is primary. It implies that the West has it completely backward. If we're lucid to it, deep, dreamless sleep—the state of utter openness—is actually when we're *most* in contact with reality. The Hindu sage Rāmana Maharshi nailed it: "That which does not exist in deep, dreamless sleep is not real." As a bow to open-minded Western thinkers, the neuroscientist Matthew Walker posits a brave hypothesis:

> Many of the explanations for why we sleep circle around a common, and perhaps erroneous idea: sleep is the state we must enter in order to fix that which has been upset by wake. But what if we turned this argument on its head? What if sleep is so useful—so physiologically beneficial to every aspect of our being—that the real question is: Why did life ever bother to wake up? Considering how biologically damaging the state of wakefulness can often be, that is the true evolutionary puzzle here. Adopt this perspective, and we can pose a very different theory: sleep was the first state of life on this planet, and it was from sleep that wakefulness emerged.[3]

Put another way, deep sleep is not the absence of consciousness; it's the consciousness of absence. But the tendency for most of us is to identify with the forms that arise in awareness (subtle thoughts and gross things), not with formless awareness (absence of forms) itself. We don't recognize dreamless sleep as a state of consciousness but as a total blackout. Because we identify with contraction, not openness; form, not emptiness; ego, not egolessness, we stay closed off to the significance of deep, dreamless sleep.

A buddha, by contrast, is someone who has opened their mind to encompass every dimension of being, not merely the waking state. "Buddha" is an epithet derived from the Sanskrit root √*budh*, meaning "to awaken" or "to open up." Buddhas are "the opened ones," while sentient beings like ourselves are "the contracted ones."[4] From our highly contracted state, openness (formlessness, emptiness, egolessness) is just too much—because it's *too little*. There is no-thing to see, so ego sees nothing.

Another reason we don't recognize deep, dreamless sleep as a state of consciousness is because we're blinded by the light of the day. Waking consciousness is a constricted state, as if we've experienced a flashbulb that temporarily blinds us. We're victims of the dominance of wake-centricity, the loudest and grossest state, which basically drowns out the other two states. The waking state is when the raucous ego is fully online, and it's imperialistically dismissive of other states it can't fully experience. Deep, dreamless sleep is just too quiet and subtle. The Buddhist scholar Reginald Ray describes our struggle to deal with the onslaught of the sensory impact we feel during waking consciousness:

> According to Tibetan Buddhism, the human ego itself is a trauma response. This is to say that experience itself, just by its very nature, when received without [contractive] filters and known directly by our Soma, is so intense and boundless that it surpasses our ego's ability to handle it and so we shut down. This goes on constantly, for all of us, just by virtue of being human . . . when we meet any new experience—and this happens in every moment—we retract, withdraw, and freeze, assimilating only a tiny fraction of what the groundless ground of our Soma knows; the rest is pushed out of awareness, down into the unconscious. [This is a] universal process by which we all as humans maintain our small sense of self, our ego, in the face of the sheer magnitude and immensity of unfiltered experience.[5]

But with meditations like the practice of open awareness, we can slow down and shut up to the point where we become familiar with these subtle states during the day and recognize them for what they truly are as they naturally unfold when we sleep. As the poet Kabir said, "What is found now is found then." Or in the untrained mind, what is *not* found now is not found then.

The next general state of consciousness manifests when the completely open, formless, and empty dimension of deep sleep contracts and condenses into the dream state. Subtle forms first manifest in this state, but the contraction is not yet complete, so the forms that arise in dreams are not as solid as those in the waking state. Things are ephemeral, fluid, and insubstantial. Because most of us are not familiar with this intermediate bandwidth of subtlety, we tend not to recognize this state of consciousness as it manifests as well, which results in the experience of normal (non-lucid) dreaming. But with meditations that correlate to this state, like dream yoga, we can become lucid dreamers, and recognize that we're dreaming while we're dreaming. We then open our minds to the wonders of the dream world.

Finally, from the partially open dimension of the dream state, consciousness contracts yet again and shrinks into the fully reified waking state.[6] (Meditators who are adept in sleep and dream yoga can witness this condensation as they come back into physical form, and the waking state, every morning. And those who are adept in liminal dreaming can watch the reverse process as they relax and dissolve into sleep every night.[7]) The waking state is the most contracted state. It's the state of consciousness we're the most familiar with—because we unwittingly *practice* contraction all the time. It's the state that we exclusively identify with, the one that is the most rock solid. Ego, which is exclusive identification with this constricted state, slams the door in the face of our deeper being, shutting out vast dimensions of the open mind and the realities dis-closed by this openness.

Ego is the most closed-minded and conservative of all states of consciousness. It's the part of us that resists new ideas—ideas like reverse meditation. If you find yourself contracting against the very notion of the challenging meditations that you'll be facing in part 2 of this book, that's your ego talking. It doesn't listen to the deepest aspects of your being, so don't listen to it. Every once in a while, the door spontaneously cracks open, which results in paranormal (para-contracted) experiences like clairvoyance, telepathy, synchronicity, intuition, and other psychic, or open-minded, phenomena, including lucid dreaming and lucid sleeping.[8]

It's because we live in the most contracted of all states that we continue to contract in everything we do. In Buddhist cosmology, we live in the *realm of desire*, which is essentially the realm of contraction.[9] We come into this world, delivered by the contractions of our mother, colossally predisposed to contract throughout the entirety of our lives. The Big Crunch itself contracts into bite-sized crunches every single time we grasp, get distracted, or hurt.

Contraction requires energy—energy that is partially drained at the end of each day, completely exhausted at the end of each life, and restored as we relax these contractions in the return to openness we call sleep and death. Contraction also creates a subliminal tension in our lives that we covertly register as existential anxiety, and overtly register as unhappiness (a topic we'll return to in chapter 9). It generates the feeling that something is missing. Something *is* missing: two-thirds of our being (sleeping and dreaming consciousness) has been squeezed out! Our longing to resolve this tension, and relieve the anxiety, manifests as our desire for happiness, which can now be seen as our yearning to return to nature—the nature of openness, and the nature of our being.

This principle of contraction, born of ultimate self-defense, is critically important in terms of understanding the necessity of bringing an integral approach to our contractions. Contraction has a place. We couldn't survive without it. We just need to find that place and keep it there. Otherwise we'll continue to inflict a heap of hurt on ourselves and others.

THE TOP TURTLES

Let's begin by exploring what I think of as the "super contractors," which I'm singling out as "super" either because of the intensity of the contraction or their omnipresent status (chapter 5). After you've been introduced to a "general contractor" (and its "subcontractors"), the discussion will be followed by some contemplations and meditations designed to sensitize you to the universal expressions of contraction. You'll be able to work your way down turtle by turtle until you arrive at the primordial contraction. These turtles are essentially suspended in open space, which is an unsettling truth that actually initiates the turtle construction project. To get to this groundless ground, we have to work our way down through all the secondary, tertiary, and quaternary iterations of contraction that serve to mask the fundamental cramp. These subordinate iterations are echoes of the primordial "Big Bang"—which in this instance is actually a Big Crunch—a squeeze that lies at the core of our sense of self.

How do these super contractors relate to the reverse meditations? By identifying the contractors, we can bring unconscious processes into the light of consciousness and reverse our relationship to them. By opening to all the ways we close, we can stay open to so much more of life and bring ourselves more fully into it.

The turtle myth is a good one for us, because if you don't look at these critters sensitively, they retract into their shell in self-defense. And self-defense is precisely the purpose of these unconscious contractions. They all serve and protect the sense of self. But we're getting ahead of ourselves. Let's work our way down to this fundamental truth one turtle at a time.

SELF-CONSCIOUSNESS

Some of the most revelatory instances of super contraction are moments of self-consciousness, which also occur along a spectrum from gross to subtle. Self-consciousness can be seen as a "general contractor," working in the construction company of the ego, along with a host of "subcontractors," such as awkwardness, embarrassment, insecurity, shyness, hesitancy, reticence, apprehension, and the like. If you want to get a feel for contraction, only a few other examples (explored below) rival the power of self-consciousness to tie you into one big knot. Self-consciousness is the mother of all contractions. We'll return to it frequently as we explore the countless ways we put the pinch on ourselves. Let's contemplate some examples of this archetypal spasm, and also use meditations to explore some of its more subtle domains.

CONTEMPLATION

Close your eyes, take a few slow, deep breaths, and relax. Check into your state of mind and body as it is right now, without changing anything and without judgment. Look and *feel* inside as if you're checking to see what the weather is like. Now bring to mind a memory of intense self-consciousness. Maybe it was a public presentation, asking a question in front of a big audience, being called out by your boss, or some form of stage fright. Maybe it was an instance of acute embarrassment. Visualize the situation as vividly as possible. Do you remember your heart pounding, your face flushing, or breaking out into a sweat? Imagine it, smell it, hear it, taste it. These exercises are only as revelatory as the effort you put into them.

For the more intrepid explorers, the sociologist Bernard McGrane offers this challenging exercise. Go to a public place, like a mall, and stand perfectly still, like a statue. Then notice the self-consciousness as people look at you, or curious children come up to you. I tried this by standing like a catatonic at the entry to a supermarket, with people streaming in and out. It was really hard to stay open, and unselfconscious, to all the strange looks I got. A security guard finally approached me, and I had to explain my totally harmless but bizarre behavior.

What do you *feel* when you touch into intense self-consciousness? A tightening in your gut? An implosion of awareness? A cascade of contractions? With this contemplation, and many to come, you're cultivating a heightened sense of your interior landscape, or *interoception*. You're gradually touching into things

> you've never touched before, bringing the unconscious into consciousness. You need to really listen to your body and feel deeply into it. That's the only way the turtles will come to the surface.

As a concert pianist and lecturer, I have lived with stage fright as a constant companion in my life. A little nervous energy is good, but I've experienced moments of intense contraction as my awareness imploded while on stage, causing me to freeze. I also used to be a competitive tennis player, and I vividly remember a particular time when I got to the finals of a club tennis tournament, one set away from victory. I reached the finals by playing in the *zone*, that marvelous flow state that is the opposite of the "anti-zone" that accompanies self-consciousness. I played out of my mind, serving aces and smacking winners from all over the court. "Out of my mind" means out of my self-conscious mind, which put me fully into the present moment. "I" (egoic self-consciousness) wasn't even there in those peak moments, and energy flowed through me effortlessly. The zone is a glimpse of selfless experience, a transcendent time zone where self-consciousness cannot enter. It's a form of meditation in action.

In the final set, with a growing gallery of spectators, the thought arose: "Hey, I could actually win this thing!" That was it. I choked. Instead of flowing through me, the energy was suddenly dammed (and damned). I became increasingly self-conscious, and by the end of the match I could barely move. Featherweight feet were replaced with lead, and I lost it—in every sense.

This is an exaggerated example of what happens at more subtle levels *all the time*. Self-consciousness, the anti-zone, rips us away from the natural state of flow, and we become children of the damned. We choke the life-force energy and fall into self-referential "think holes" that are deeper and darker than any black hole.

CONTEMPLATION

What can we do about these contracted states? First, celebrate that you can even touch into the contraction, which now allows you to relate to it. Then reverse your relationship and stay with the contraction, but without judgment. Don't try to get rid of it. Make friends with it. The simple act of being with it starts to transform it.

Second, be curious and inquisitive. Allow yourself to go into the self-consciousness fully, to really feel it. Get in touch with the sensation as completely as you can. Sometimes you can investigate exactly where you feel the sensation in your body. But don't get too analytic. Keep your conceptual mind in check.

Third, breathe into it, open up to it. Allow the contracted feeling to ventilate. This won't necessarily dissolve it, but it creates a new context of openness. It reframes the experience by placing it in a greater context.

Finally, when the storylines begin their inevitable commentary, let the narrative go, and return to the felt sense. Stay in your body. Your body knows what to do with this feeling. If you stay embodied, the feeling naturally self-liberates. Each of these steps will be unpacked in detail when we explore the formal reverse meditations, but this will get you started.

ANGER AND AGGRESSION

Anger, aggression, and their many subcontractors—rage, wrath, fury, indignation, bitterness, resentment, enmity, and animosity—are high on the list of super contractors. Nothing makes me feel more solid and real than anger. My body tenses, my hands clench into fists, and my heart pounds. Anger and aggression are among the most reconstituting of all emotions. Their ability to solidify the self helps me understand the outbursts that occur when things fall apart, and instills a sense of empathy when others are losing it. I spend a fair amount of time with those who are dying, and their caretakers. It's common in situations of disintegration for people to lash out in anger, even at caregivers. When things are coming unglued, anger often rears its head as a superglue to keep it all together. By understanding what's happening, we won't take it personally.

Anger and aggression are territorial, and they trigger defensive or offensive reactions to protect our turf. The most intimate territory, which must be defended at all costs, is the terrain of the self, and all that is included in the field of I, me, and mine. When something gets too close to home—and the ultimate home is my body and the sense of self it houses—I'll contract to defend this most personal property.

CONTEMPLATION

Settle your mind with a few deep breaths, and feel into your body as before. Now tune in to some news program that really makes you angry or annoys the beans out of you. If you're a liberal Democrat, watch Fox News and people like Sean Hannity or Tucker Carlson. If you're a conservative Republican, watch MSNBC and people like Rachel Maddow or Chris Hayes. This reverse exercise is sure to get your goat.

Feel the contraction of your anger or annoyance, and see if you can stay open to it. Notice how easy it is to get defensive, and criticize or complain, when you tense up. How can we ever expect to heal the culture wars, or relate to those with vastly different views, if we can't stay open to others?

As a refinement of this practice, you can add what I'll call the "mute meditation." I stumbled upon this during the Brett Kavanaugh Supreme Court hearings, when the histrionics captivated the nation. While I was watching it one day, getting more and more sucked into the drama, I spontaneously reached out to hit the mute button. Within a second everything changed. Kavanaugh was still there, flushed and gesticulating wildly, but watching the display without sound stripped it of its power. I found myself less contracted, and chuckled at the theater of it all.

The practice is to watch someone who gets you riled up, like Maddow or Hannity, then hit the mute button on your reactivity. Notice how your contraction relaxes. Next, use the same "silencer" approach in your meditation. In other words, when some reactive storyline is racing through your mind and getting you all worked up, whether you're on the meditation cushion or in daily life, hit the mute button on your mind. Don't listen to the narrative. The mental display is still there, just like on silent TV, but you're no longer buying into it.

FEAR AND PANIC

Fear and panic—along with their cousins anxiety, worry, trepidation, alarm, suspicion, mistrust, concern, agitation, dread, and shock—join the short list of super contractors. When I touch into moments of fear in my life, I'm touching into something super solid. Even in moments of harmless surprise, my awareness implodes to generate a highly centralized feeling. Fear protects form, and it constellates a healthy level of contraction to ensure physical survival. When your body is threatened, fearful contraction can save your life.

But as evolution continues beyond physical form, as proclaimed by philosophers like Teilhard de Chardin, the very fear that developed to safeguard evolution now comes to retard it. Ego is a stage in human evolution, they suggest, characterized by exclusive identification with form. On the path of psychological and spiritual development, we aspire to grow beyond ego—we aspire to transcend our exclusive identification with form. On the spiritual path, in particular, we evolve from ego to egolessness, from form to formlessness, and this evolution can be interpreted as a death threat by the fully formed ego. Fear is the mood of self-contraction, and a central player on the path of evolution. An integral approach is in order—honoring the place of fear in evolution, and then keeping it in its place.

Anger and fear are two of the principal ways we solidify our experience. Anger reifies the past, and fear reifies the future. By understanding this, we can dereify our anger and fear, which also dereifies the past and future, delivering us into the only place that truly exists—the present.

CONTEMPLATION

Bring to mind a frightening experience. Maybe it was being alone at night when the power suddenly went off or hearing a thump in the dark. Notice the self-contraction, and the corresponding solidity of this emotion. The next time you're startled or spooked, notice how instantly you contract, like when you're cut off on the road or suddenly lose your footing.

As a reverse meditation for addressing fear, the Tibetan meditation master Khenpo Tsültrim Gyamtso Rinpoche did extensive retreats in the charnel grounds of India and Tibet. Charnel grounds are traditionally the most horrific environments you can imagine: places where bodies are left outside to rot, and where vultures and hyenas feed on the corpses. The equivalent today might be doing a meditation retreat at an ER in a big city, a site of ecological devastation, a war zone, or a place of natural disaster.

To simulate the flavor of meditation that can be accomplished in these fearful spaces, Rinpoche recommended that his students watch horror movies. I've done this practice, and initially I found it silly. Horror films are repulsive, stupid, and . . . highly contractive. To bring any sense of practice to these viewings, I often had to hit not merely the mute button but the pause button. As contrived as this approach may be, it did give me the opportunity to work with a host of unwanted feelings. Try it, and notice where you feel the reactions in your body. Then stay embodied. Feel the contractions, but don't feed them.

CHAPTER 5

THE OMNIPRESENT SUPER CONTRACTORS

In order to manifest as a world, consciousness contracts
within itself. . . . In order for consciousness to reclaim its
innate happiness, a reversal of this process takes place.

—RUPERT SPIRA

We live inside a self-woven conceptual cocoon
that insulates us from raw reality.

—BERNARDO KASTRUP

A notch below the overt and forceful super contractors of self-consciousness, anger and aggression, and fear and panic, we find constrictions that may seem less powerful but are more omnipresent. These include criticism and complaint, with their many subcontractors—quibble, lament, wail, moan, reprimand, harangue, disapprove, protest, dispute, blame, or censure. Closely allied are the many forms of gossip and slander (defamation, denigration, denunciation, deprecation, humiliation) that express these contractions. Criticism and complaint are not just overt and external, or always directed toward others. They're equally internal, often directed toward ourselves. Monitor your own mind and you'll see how hard you can be on yourself.

The more subtle the contraction, the more omnipresent it tends to be. The most subtle of all contractions are the most constant. According to Buddhist psychology, they occur even as we sleep. Discovering the ubiquitous nature of these midrange contractions continues to humble me. I take my dog for a walk, notice the poop left by a careless neighbor's dog, and contract in self-righteous aversion. A minute later someone walks by who won't acknowledge me, and I contract with a critical thought. A minute later it starts to drizzle, eliciting yet another complaint. Then I fulminate about the crazy cost of the plumber back at the house, the annoying sound of the leaf blower, or the decision I don't agree with at the Supreme Court.

CONTEMPLATION

Take a break and go for a walk. Without judging yourself, see if you can keep track of all the times you contract in criticism or complaint about what you experience during the walk—be honest with yourself. Or take a drive, and track your contractions. Does that rude driver make you contract? Or that political billboard? Or the litter on the side of the road?

The following "anticomplaint meditation" is a practice I use daily: the next time you feel the urge to complain, pause for a moment; then ask yourself, "What am I feeling right now that I just don't want to feel?" Every time I do this, I discover some unwanted feeling in my body, along with the immediate contraction that attempts to keep me from feeling it. The contraction squirts me out of my feeling body and into my thinking head, which leads me to feel less and think more.

The next part of this anticomplaint practice is to boycott the storylines in your head and to drop back into your body. Complaining is a kind of out-of-body experience. You've left the unwanted sensation in your body, and you've exited into your concepts. You've lost touch with what's happening. If the feeling is really unwanted, you might temporarily lose your mind as you lash out. The practice is to notice the impulse to eject out of the feeling—then *reverse* that impulse, and stay embodied.

This practice is an instance of "waking down" (instead of waking up) and staying with the contraction. It lets you reconnect to the underlying feeling, which allows the feeling to self-liberate into pure (and often intense) energy. The practice of open awareness in part 2 of this book, and the reverse meditations that follow, train you to tolerate more and more intense experience without contracting. As Rumi said, "Flow down and down and down, in ever-widening rings of being." The mind becomes "wider" as it *descends* and opens, until it expands to accommodate everything.

REACTIVITY AND JUDGMENT

The list of omnipresent super contractors has to include reactivity and judgment. Just look at how often you react to things or judge yourself and others. On a biological level, you can tune in to healthy reactivity or contraction when you step off the curb and an oncoming car blasts its horn to keep you out of harm's way. If it's a really close call, and your reaction is correspondingly intense, you can be shaken for hours by the force of that contraction. Any instance of shock delivers a contractive punch that can reverberate for years, as in PTSD. When I get a dreaded phone call that someone close to me has died, or I'm unexpectedly fired, or the doctor tells me the lab report isn't good, the experience slams into me with such force that my whole being is stunned by the level of contraction.

I'm constantly reacting to the events in my life, and now that I'm sensitized to how synonymous reactivity is with contraction, I can bring reactivity onto the path and replace it with response-ability. Reactivity is self-centered. Response-ability is reality (or other) centered. In other words, responses are more open and receptive to what's happening. Response-ability is not based on how everything relates to me. I still need to function and relate to things, but I can do so responsibly. A responsive relationship allows me to stay in touch with what's happening, and with others, without the usual "profit mentality" of my reactions: "How can *I* benefit from this event?" "What does this situation mean to *me*?" "What can *I* get from this person?"

Self-centeredness is one of the reasons we keep on reacting. Self-centeredness sustains the ego construction project. So we react, biologically and psychologically, as if our lives depended on it—because they do. Contraction creates and preserves our physical and psychological sense of self. We rely on contractions to "help us avoid unlimited increases of entropy in our internal states," according to Bernardo Kastrup:

> If we saw the world as it actually is, if our perception mirrored the world as it actually is, then our internal states would be as unbound as the states of the world. That means that seeing alone could kill you. It could increase the dispersion of your internal states to the point that you would melt into hot soup (that's thermodynamics for you). It has been shown mathematically that perception *cannot* mirror the world; we would die very quickly if it did that. Perception is an encoded, at a glance, overview of what is salient and relevant about the world [for our survival].[1]

Our integral approach, which honors the healthy role of contraction in life, allows us to include contraction when it's necessary for survival, while also transcending contraction when it starts to hold us back.

CONTEMPLATION

Let's return to our Sean Hannity and Rachel Maddow exercise. If political commentary doesn't put a burr under your saddle, try watching a religious personality, perhaps a fundamentalist with a worldview vastly removed from your own. Do you feel the reactivity and judgment, and how it affects your ability to listen? Do you find yourself formulating a response before the person on your screen even completes a sentence?

Now hit the mute button for a minute. Then unmute, and see if you can stay open to what you're hearing. Can you respond to what's being said with equanimity, understanding, and even compassion? Can you stay open to what you're hearing, without buying in to what is being said?

Every judgment comes with a flicker of contraction. For those on the meditative path, "judgment day" is every day. The yoga master Swami Kripalu said, "The highest form of spiritual practice is self-observation without judgment." To which we can add: the highest form of spiritual practice is *any* observation without judgment. This doesn't mean we lose our ability for healthy discrimination, or for discerning right from wrong, but rather that we learn to open to things with equanimity, which allows us to act responsibly.

We learn to say "yes" to whatever arises, as a valid part of our experience, then respond from that receptive stance in more skillful ways. Which sometimes requires saying "no." Saying "yes" to whatever occurs also acknowledges the sacredness of that occurrence, before the profanity of self-referential commentary barges in. Our actions then become reality-centered instead of self-centered. We act for the inclusive benefit of others, instead of the exclusive benefit of ourselves.

GRASPING AND ATTACHMENT

Two key propensities most readily reveal the omnipresence of contraction: the active display of grasping, and the passive expression of grasping as attachment. Contraction is more fundamental than grasping, but grasping—and its infinite iterations, like craving, passion, lust, greed, hoarding, possessiveness, miserliness, desire, longing, impatience, ambition, hunger, or thirst—is one of contraction's most ubiquitous manifestations. And because we know that ego is the archetype of contraction, it follows to say that grasping is *ego*'s most inexorable expression, virtually synonymous with it.

Ultimately, then, to end contraction is to trans*cend* the ego, which is why so much of the spiritual path is about letting go. The challenge we experience in attempting to let go reveals how much we love to grasp. It's stunning how difficult it is to release our emotional grip, even though grasping causes so much suffering. But like other contractions, grasping is in service to preserving the ego—and for the ego, an existence that involves suffering is better than no existence at all.

The Buddhist view that we live in the realm of desire is a recognition of this egoic situation, that we live in the realm of grasping and attachment. We live in a realm of wanting. But why do we want? Because we feel that something is missing or wanting. We feel empty inside, an ineffable sense of lack. This is deficient emptiness, not the fullness of emptiness (śūnyāta) introduced earlier. We're not sure why we feel this lack, but we grasp to fill the insatiable void.

What do we grasp? Forms—physical, mental, and spiritual. We contract around things, phenomena that are themselves the result of the even more fundamental contraction that creates the sense of thingness altogether—the primordial contraction at the bottom of all those turtles in chapter 4 (a concept we'll talk about more fully in chapter 6). In other words, even the sense of "thing," of some*thing* to grasp, is the result of contraction itself. Contractions contracting onto other contractions—all the way up and down.

CONTEMPLATION

Take a few slow breaths and settle into your body. The more you relax and open, the more you'll be able to feel the subtle closures. Now bring to mind someone you crave or something that you really want. Visualize that person or object as vividly as possible: imagining, smelling, hearing, tasting, touching. Get into the visualization. What do you *feel* when you touch into strong desire? Do you feel your body constricting as awareness shrinks around the object?

The contractions are often literal, like when we clutch that desired person in our arms, inhale the smoke from that treasured cigarette, or grab that cherished object. On more subtle levels, we savor the delight of grasping an idea, getting a grip on a complex problem, or seizing an opportunity. One of the reasons we might not see these contractions, and the more subtle ones to follow, is because of their constancy. There's no contrast, no break. If you're doing something all the time, it's easy to forget that you're doing it. It starts to "do" you.

Acute clenching readily petrifies into chronic fixation. Attachment is a form of frozen or solidified grasping. It's more difficult to detect because it's even more constant and subliminal. We're attached to countless things: our views, ideas, opinions, politics, philosophies, assumptions, beliefs, hopes, fears, thoughts, emotions, feelings, perceptions, and possessions. The untamed mind sticks to absolutely everything.

One of the most literal and foundational attachments is how stuck we are on ourselves, including our body. One teacher said that enlightenment is the ultimate "getting over yourself." According to the Tibetan teachings on death and dying, this attachment is so elemental that when our body is removed from us at death, we'll grasp after another one with such desperation that it will hurl us into our next body in a process of endless rebirth.[2] Contraction in the service of rebirth takes place at many levels, from literal to figurative, acute to chronic, overt to covert.

Habituated contractions manifest as addictions. The neuroscientist Judson Brewer, in his book *The Craving Mind: From Cigarettes to Smartphones to Love—Why We Get Hooked & How We Can Break Bad Habits*, shows how we're addicted to technology, distraction, thinking, love, and ourselves. We're addicted to so many things—including the notion of "thing" itself. And we get our "fix" by capitulating to all our fixations.

Our levels of attachment are painfully revealed when something is taken away. That's when our fingers are pried open, releasing a grip we forgot we even had. When a beloved object is destroyed or stolen, or when someone close to us gets sick or dies, only then do we register how fixated we are. The disclosure is often shocking and manifests as various levels of grief. It may seem cold to proclaim this harsh truth, but our level of grief is directly proportional to our level of attachment. Grief is a form of withdrawal. If we're not attached, we can relate to impermanence with equanimity. If we're really attached, impermanence (the most common expression of emptiness) can be devastating. This doesn't mean we shouldn't care for the objects in our lives, and love the people who are close to us, but that we can love without attachment. Then, when the inevitable losses of life occur, we're not as adversely affected.

CONTEMPLATION

The following contemplation is part of the bardo—or preparatory practices for death—in the Tibetan tradition, and it's not easy. On five separate pieces of paper, write down the five most important physical objects in your life. For me, these are my grand piano, my library of books, all my albums and recordings, my house, and my computer. Whatever they are, bring them into your mind and heart and reflect on how important they are to you. Hold each piece of paper, then tear it to shreds, and say "death" as you rip it apart.

Next, take five more pieces of paper and write down the five most treasured people (or pets) in your life. Bring them into your mind and heart as above. Pause, and touch into their limitless value. Reflect on the beautiful memories you have with them and how much joy they have brought to you. Now rip these pieces of paper apart, and say "death" as you do so.

When I do this exercise in my seminars, it often elicits gasps, and then tears. Everything we're attached to will disappear or die, and our level of attachment will be painfully exposed. This is not to judge how attached we are but to reveal our degree of attachment. This is not to dismiss the preciousness of the objects and people that make life worth living but to put things in perspective and to help us understand why we grieve.

STRESS AND TENSION

Two more principal manifestations of contraction are acute stress and chronic tension, along with their infinite iterations including distress, strain, worry, unease, disquietude, concern, burden, encumbrance, and apprehension. Stress is almost synonymous with life in the modern world, and a leading contributor to mental and physical disease. Like so many psychological states, stress eventually downloads into the body. At the most overt level, stress becomes frozen into our body armor, distorting our posture. Stress leads to chronic muscle contraction, resulting in hunched shoulders, furrowed brows, clenched jaws, muscle-tension headaches, and a cascade of stress disorders. When I was in clinical practice as a dentist, and patients came in with a host of oral-facial diseases, top on my list of diagnostic questions was, "How is your stress these days?"

At a more covert level, stress and tension find their way to the cellular level. Until we do opening and stretching exercises, we may have no idea how physically contracted we are. When I started yoga, I was almost shocked by my inability to even approximate the postures. I was the Tin Man from the *Wizard of Oz*, robotic in my inflexibility.

Reginald Ray, a leading Buddhist practitioner of somatic awareness meditation, summarizes this experience of how stress manifests in countless levels of tension in the mind and body:

> As we become more and more aware of the parts of our body, at a certain point we will notice something else: the tension in each part. The more we explore this, the more we begin to sense that our entire body is actually riddled with tension. We are talking here not about the natural, healthy tension that is part of being human, but instead we are talking about neurotic tension, elective tension, superimposed tension—superimposed by our conscious orientation, our ego. Neurobiology tells us that this kind of pathological tension extends all the way down to the cellular level and is a contributing factor to ill health and disease.[3]

CONTEMPLATION

Bring to mind a pressing deadline, a worrisome memory, or the recollection of a stressful event. Think about the stressfulness of that situation in terms of contraction; try to locate the contraction and be very specific as to where you notice it. Do you sense it in your gut? Do you feel it in your heart? Do you register it in your head? See where these sensations take you. Does your entire body feel like one big knot? Only when you see how wound up you really are can you begin to unwind. The knots are actually "nots." Each knot is tied every time we say "no" to experience and reject what's happening. If we can replace rejection with acceptance, we gradually release all these knots.

For instance, I'm writing this book during the peak of the COVID-19 pandemic, intense political polarization, and social unrest. Like contraction itself, life these days is layer upon layer of stress. I often don't feel all these layers until I do my daily yoga or meditation, and I recognize them as they melt away. Sometimes the contrast is dramatic—from a contracted body-mind at the beginning of my meditation session to deep relaxation at the end.

As you continue to get a feel for your contractions, you'll start to discover them on your own. "Oh my! There's another one! I had no idea I was so contracted." The diagnosis always precedes the prescription. The good news is that the antidote to all of them is simple. Open and relax. But simple isn't always easy. It is theoretically possible to release them all by going after the primordial contraction (and I promise we'll get to more on that). Just relax the primordial cramp, and every other contraction collapses like a falling house of cards. But the directness is proportional to the difficulty. For most people, it's easier to remove the cards one by one.

DISTRACTION

Our list of super contractors wouldn't be complete without including distraction. Every single time we get distracted, we're contracting away from the present moment. We're pulling away from what's happening in our sensitive body, which is always in the present moment, and squirting up into our insensible head. Just walk through a public place to witness the alarming pandemic of distraction, as people hypnotized by their smart phones trip over things and bump into others.

Hinduism and Buddhism both predicted the Kali Yuga, or Dark Age, the era that we find ourselves in today. What makes the Dark Age so dark is its insidious nature, and its subversive ability to take down entire civilizations without the citizens realizing that the collapse is happening. The dark virus infecting us is so subtle that few people realize they're afflicted with it. Distracted people don't notice things—like the fact that they're so distracted. The cartoon character SpongeBob, in a humorous segment when the lights suddenly go out, anxiously quips: "This isn't your everyday darkness. . . . This is *advanced darkness!*" What makes the darkness of our age so advanced is that it occurs not when the lights go out, but when they go on—and never turn off.

The advent of artificial light, and our addiction to it, marks the formal beginning of the Kali Yuga. Images from outer space reveal that light pollution is accelerating at alarming rates, adversely affecting our planet.[4] Images from those who venture into inner space—the mystics and contemplatives—reveal a similarly disconcerting effect on the human psyche. Artificial light pulls us away from ourselves, distracting us from our true nature, blinding us to who we really are, and creating loads of anxiety that we try to deaden with more distraction. The seventeenth-century philosopher Blaise Pascal could not even have begun to imagine the electronic diversions of centuries to come when he wrote,

> The only thing that consoles us for our miseries is diversion. And yet it is the greatest of our miseries. For it is that above all which prevents us thinking about ourselves and leads us imperceptibly to destruction. But for that we should be bored, and boredom would drive us to seek some more solid means of escape, but diversion passes our time and brings us imperceptibly to our death. . . . I have discovered that all the unhappiness of men arises from one simple fact, that they cannot stay quietly in their own chamber.[5]

Pascal offered the remedy centuries ago, and we'll accept his invitation to "stay quietly in our own chamber," the chamber of the present moment, when we engage the meditations that act as the vaccine to this raging pandemic.

THE SUPER EXPANDERS

In the spirit of alchemy and tantra, if we're armed with the proper view, and practices like open awareness and the reverse meditations, the super contractors that we have been describing can transform into "super expanders." That which previously closed us down can be used to open us up. It is possible, whenever we feel self-consciousness, anger or aggression, fear or panic, complaint or criticism, reactivity or judgment, grasping or attachment, stress or tension, to use that contraction as an opportunity to open. There is so much grist for this mill!

The reverse meditations in part 2 of this book mostly derive from the tantric tradition, which is called "the quick path." Tantra is considered to be among the highest teachings in Buddhism and Hinduism, unique in its ability to bring meditation into daily life. One reason tantra is quick is because *everything* becomes the path. Another reason is that experiences that previously hindered our path now accelerate it. That's a dealmaker. By reversing our strategies, and going directly into all these contracted states, the energies trapped within them are released and transformed into the rocket fuel for your journey. So fasten your seat belt, and prepare to boldly go where you have never gone before. Nowhere. Or fully into the now-here.

CHAPTER 6

CHARACTERISTICS OF CONTRACTION

The task is to bring the process back to the
initial point, before any "superimpositions" have
distorted the actual and initial datum.

—EDWARD CONZE

And they understood that there's no going up without
going down, no heaven without going through
hell. . . . Everything had to be experienced, included:
and to find clarity meant facing utter darkness.

—PETER KINGSLEY

Our tendency to contract has been present from birth. And because the tendency is so automatic, constant, and unconscious, contraction seems natural to us. It's our default, the undetected baseline of our being. But contraction is not at all natural, and not in any way who we truly are. Terence McKenna's phrase "lethal cultural adaptation" could be repurposed to talk about "lethal individual adaptation"— adapting to something for so long that it is no longer discernible as an adaptation, but instead it's become axiomatic, a given. It's like the proverbial frog, placed in warming waters, that slowly gets boiled alive as it adapts to the rising temperatures. Proper adaptation is the key to evolution, but lethal adaptation is the key to extinction.

Bio-physical contraction is healthy and natural—it literally saves our skins. But psycho-spiritual contraction is an artificial and synthetic process. It's the first step in a sophisticated construction project and avoidance strategy. Layer upon layer of adaptation has extinguished our contact with reality. At foundational levels, contraction localizes the infinite mind to the space-time coordinates of the finite body. It shrink-wraps infinity and eternity into bite-sized chunks so the ego, which fully identifies with the body, can digest what's happening. This primordial contraction is actually a secondary phenomenon, a defensive event that protects the ego from the harsh absolute truths that underlie the contraction.

Reginald Ray explains egoic defenses in this way:

> Any naked, unfiltered experience is initially felt to be painful and problematic; without thinking, we try to withdraw from it, evade and get away from it. We do so by literally tensing up, and this tension is everywhere. Why is unfiltered experience painful? Because any new experience is perceived by the conscious ego as a threat. As William Blake observed, human experience in its primary, unprocessed form is infinite. This infinity runs against one of the ego's primary functions, which is to meet the unexpected and, through subverting it into a convenient and safe interpretive framework, to limit and control it and finally, when carried to an extreme, to deny not only its significance but its very existence. When new meditators confess, "I feel so locked up, I don't even know what my life is" or "I feel like I am missing out on the experience of being alive," they speak the truth. Tensing up is a way of avoiding the unadorned experience and the discomfort it brings ego, whether that discomfort is

physical or psychological; tension is our way of closing down experience and shutting off awareness.[1]

One of the unconscious ways that ego filters reality is through predictive processing, in which organisms are "fundamentally anticipatory," according to the neuroscientists Ruben Laukkonen and Heleen Slagter. Organisms are "continuously inferring or predicting the outside world based on prior experience." The researchers suggest that "due to the fact that the brain lacks direct access to the external world, it must 'guess' or predict the hidden causes of sensory input based on past experience in order to adaptively interact with it."[2] In other words, perception is basically the brain's best guess as to what's out there—a bad guess that dramatically reduces the infinite bombardment of unfiltered experience into something we can relate to.

Not only do we perceive mere snippets of reality when the filtering is done, but as part of this contractive and reductive process, we also *project* what is inside of us outside. This projection of misleading signals serves to further filter out reality, like a self-protecting cocoon. The physicist Carlo Rovelli writes:

> Many, if not most, of the signals do not travel from the eyes to the brain; they go the other way, from the brain to the eyes. What happens is that the brain *expects* to see something, on the basis of what it knows and has previously occurred. The brain elaborates an image of what it *predicts* the eyes should see. This information is conveyed *from* the brain *to* the eyes, through intermediate stages. If a discrepancy is revealed between what the brain expects and the light arriving into the eyes, *only then* do the neural circuits send signals toward the brain. So images from around us do not travel from the eyes to the brain—only news of discrepancies regarding what the brain expects do. . . . What I see, in other words, is not a reproduction of the external world. It is what I expect, corrected by what I can grasp.[3]

What I see is corrected and filtered by what the ego can bear. But this "correction" is, in fact, a corruption. It's a distortion of what's really happening. This process twists reality as it truly is into our "corrected" and contracted version of what it should be—of what we expect it to be. The French philosopher Hippolyte Taine said that "external perception is an internal dream which proves to be in harmony with external things; and instead of calling 'hallucination' a false perception, we must call external perception 'a confirmed hallucination'"[4]—a confirmed hallucination created by contraction, both of which operate on neurological, perceptual, cognitive, developmental, and psychological levels.

By unearthing the features of contraction—and other steps in the construction project that builds out the ego (and by immediate implication, the external world)—we can boycott the construction of self and begin the process of demolition. This understanding is central to deconstructing not just the ego but also all the suffering that ensues from this construction-contraction project. It's not philosophical indulgence but doctrinal footing that empowers us to engage the following deconstructing meditations. Even though the edifice built by well-established layers of contraction is imposing, the entire project can be analyzed and taken apart.

A "divide and conquer" approach—identifying, and gradually releasing, the characteristics of contraction that co-conspire to create our cramped lives—is one of two ways to relax our contractions. It's the relative approach we've been taking so far, where we slowly but surely unravel all the compressions one by one, working our way back to the primordial compactor—and then below that into open reality. The absolute approach, which we'll emphasize in later chapters, is faster and simpler: just open and relax. Ease the primary cramp, and all the secondary contractions dissolve. But because the primordial contraction is so far down, so constant, and so long-standing, it's not easy to access or release. The primordial contraction is so solid, so deep in our unconscious mind, that we don't even feel that we don't feel. So we'll continue the releasing process by working with more accessible contractions.

It may initially appear that "I" am the one doing all the contracting. This is a partial truth. Many of the secondary, tertiary, quaternary, and subsequent contractions are indeed the result of activities done in service of the self. But the very sense of self is the *result* of contraction. It's not just contraction in the service of the self, but contraction as the generation of the self. The primordial contraction generates the sense of self, which then spins an endless web of secondary contractions to further solidify itself. Let's return to the construction site by unearthing the principal characteristics of contraction and then offering the antidotes to them.

ACTIVE

The first characteristic of contraction is that it is an active process, more a verb (contracting) than a noun. Even the primordial contraction, which can seem as solid as a block of ice, is a vibrant process, always in need of refrigeration. Reflecting on her own life experience, the spiritual teacher Deborah Eden Tull captures the high-maintenance nature of contractions and the consequent way they trap our energy:

> This habit of *pushing away* the difficult stuff, which seemed to keep popping back up no matter how hard I tried to push it down, was exhausting. I worked to maintain a positive self-image and was appreciated for being a "bright light," yet that light did not include the whole of me. My pain was kept secret instead of made sacred.[5]

If we didn't constantly feed our contractions, they would wither away. When contraction is associated with distraction, we see how much time and energy, or "food," they consume. Meditation is a form of fasting that starves our contractions. With the upcoming meditations, we'll learn how to feel, but not feed, our insatiable appetites to grasp/contract.

Contraction is like a spinning top. If you don't keep adding to the momentum, it topples over. The continual maintenance of our contractions is why so much energy is released once we stop contracting, and why relaxation alone can unwind every contraction. Relaxation is the ultimate deactivator, a one-size-fits-all remedy. It's the easiest thing in the world—which, paradoxically, is what makes it so hard. Just do nothing. But do it really well. Meditate. And remember the Taoist adage: "By doing nothing, nothing is left undone."

Keep these core instructions in mind as we progress into what might initially appear to be a host of subtle and multifaceted meditations. The intricacy of these meditations is designed to meet the complexity of the modern mind, which just can't buy that the solution is really this simple. On an absolute level, you don't need any of the following information or the practices that implement it. Just open and relax. That's it. But when people hear this modest instruction, they tend to reply, "Yes . . . but." That's the complex mind stepping in. If you find yourself disputing the simplicity and saying "but," then we have this thing called the path.

If you don't want to open and relax now, watch this relaxation occur on nature's nonnegotiable terms when you die. Death is just forced openness, an uncompromising way to rest in peace. In this context, deep meditation, especially the practice of open awareness, is just death in slow motion—unwinding before you're forced to do so. Everything comes undone when you die. There's finally nothing left to do. And the result of doing nothing so well (as in deep meditation or death), if one can recognize it for what it is, is the Grand Opening, or enlightenment.

Think of an EF4 tornado, which can reach winds over three hundred miles per hour and strip the bark off a tree. That's a tremendous amount of pent-up energy. Now imagine your body-mind as riddled with such cyclones—in the form of stress and tension, along with all the other contractors—and consider all the internal damage those cyclones cause. Think about how they are the source of so much mental and physical dis-ease, and try to fathom all the energy they consume.[6]

Bernardo Kastrup offers the image of "mind at large" (which refers to the infinite stream of consciousness beyond our personal mind) as a stream, and asks us to picture a whirlpool in this stream, which represents the ego, or self-sense. The spinning vortex serves to contract and localize some of the water, trapping it into place as it swirls around a specific (but empty) center. The whirlpool appropriates some of the water, grasping after the ungraspable (the infinite flux of the stream), in a twisted attempt to make it its own. Offering images that align with others who have suggested the filtered nature of reality, Kastrup writes, "Just like the whirlpool can be said to 'filter out' the water molecules that do not get trapped in it, we can say that the brain 'filters out' the aspects of reality—that is, experiences—that do not fall within its own boundaries."[7]

When you wake up in the middle of the night and can't fall back asleep, doesn't the dizzying mental content make you feel like you're stuck in a merry-go-round that isn't all that merry? When you're alone with your mind, doesn't it seem like there's an endless stream of thoughts spinning around you? This is one way to feel the active force (wind) of your contractions. The central whirlpool, which represents our self-sense, has smaller whirlpools within it, just as a big wave can have smaller waves on its surface, or a fractal has iterative images within it. We experience these smaller whirlpools whenever we get sucked into thoughts, or when we find ourselves spinning into endless self-sustaining storylines. The whirlpool represents how we get all wrapped up in ourselves, often spinning out of control. But if you don't invest attention in these mental twisters, if you stop feeding them, they gradually decelerate and disintegrate. The Indian guru Sri Nisargadatta Maharaj said, "It is disinterestedness that liberates."

The velocity of the spin dictates the solidity of the sense of self. When we're all wound up, we can feel as solid as a rock, and the world seems correlatively hard. When we slow down and relax, the world magically responds in kind. Everything now feels softer. But what most of us do not see, until we start to meditate, are the unconscious levels of just how wound up we are, how we tie ourselves into knots on so many levels. When beginning meditators complain that meditation seems to be making things worse, it's because they had never slowed down long enough before to see the speed of the spin.

Here's another analogy. Reach out and touch space. When you're silent and still, it's the softest thing in the world. But get into a Ferrari, slam the pedal to the metal, put your hand out of the window, and that space can now rip your arm off. Speed (wind) turns the softest thing in the universe into concrete. The ego feeds on speed and acts as a kind of hovercraft kept aloft through the speed of its spin, the propeller of samsāra, that keeps us hovering above the empty nature of reality—and just out of touch with what's really happening. Ego generates the illusion of ground—solidity— through speed. It's the only way to "freeze" space long enough to give the ego a place to stand.

When we unwind in deep meditation, fall asleep, or die, the finite whirlpool relaxes and dissolves back into the infinite stream of consciousness from which it arose. The unwinding has neurological signatures when we fall asleep, in a progression that can be measured by an EEG. From high-energy gamma frequencies (25-100 hz), we decelerate to beta wavelengths (12-25 hz), then reduce speed down to alpha (8-12 hz), then slow down further into the relaxed states of theta (4-8 hz), until we come to a full stop in the deep, dreamless state of delta (0-4 hz). You can witness this unwinding in the peaceful countenance of someone when they're sound asleep in delta, with a face so open and relaxed it almost looks divine.

Death, in relation to wind, is the ultimate un-winding—as exemplified when you literally take your last breath. "Physical death is the partial image of the process of unraveling the egoic loop," says Kastrup. "But it is conceivable that the psychic structure entails an underlying, partial, not-so-tightly-closed loop underneath the egoic loop." From this premise, he concludes, "Assuming that physical death entails the dissolution of only the egoic loop on top, then our awareness would 'fall back' onto the underlying partial loop, preserving a degree of self-reflectiveness."[8] The whirlpool dissolves, but the stream never ends.

We can expand on the whirlpool image to explore another dynamic feature of contraction: pulsation. Try to imagine a whirlpool that has a pulse. Contractions relax and open, allowing us to make brief contact with reality, but then quickly tighten back up. They contract as a way to feed information back to central headquarters—just enough data for us to survive. If we didn't have some semblance of contact with reality, some degree of openness, we'd be totally frozen, as in catatonia, or more common moments of intense self-consciousness. Have you ever been so self-conscious that you could barely function?

The stream image, meanwhile, is useful for thinking about "flow" states, which occur when we relax self-consciousness and ride the current of reality, instead of contracting against it (as I did during my experience of entering the zone while playing that tennis tournament). Contractions dam the natural flow of life and often make us feel stuck. We dam ourselves (or damn ourselves) every time we put the squeeze on the effulgence of life and the flow of life-energy. By breaking this dam through meditation, we open the flow and open to the understanding that we too are but a stream within a stream. The ecologist Joanna Macy writes that she has learned to see herself in terms used by systems theorists—as a "flow-through," declaring "I am a flow through of matter, energy, and information."

In one of the oldest of Buddhist traditions, the orthodox teachings known as Theravada Buddhism, opening to the flow of reality is suggested in the stage of practice called "entering the stream" (*sottāpana* in Pali), which is the first of four stages on the path to enlightenment in that tradition.[9] A sottāpana is a "stream-enterer," someone who has stepped outside the whirlpool. You enter the stream when you open the eye of dharma ("truth"), which is the moment of seeing that there's more to reality than mere appearance—there's more to life than being trapped in a whirlpool. Another rendering of "entering the stream" occurs by cutting the "three fetters," in which the first fetter is the belief in the self—our exclusive identification with the whirlpool.[10] A central characteristic of a stream is to flow, and anything that enters a stream will be carried along with it. Entering the stream, therefore, refers to entering the stream of dharma, of reality, and being carried away by the truth as it moves you to enlightenment. The practitioner releases the flow of life-force energy rather than damming up that energy through constant self-reference.

To introduce yet another metaphor, the contraction of self-referencing can be thought of as gravitational pull. Like the planets in our solar system orbiting the sun, everything in our lives orbits a narrative center of gravity—*me*. As long as we have an ego, everything is self-centered. Doesn't it seem like the same old thoughts and emotions keep spinning around us? How about the revolving patterns of our lives? Isn't it all about me? I've heard a psychologist estimate that 90 percent of the thoughts we have today are the same thoughts we had yesterday. How does this situation relate to *me*, what can *I* get out of this, where do *I* fit in, am *I* okay? On one level, we need this self-centeredness in order to physically survive. But on another level, self-centricity breeds ego-centricity and all our self-referential suffering. The twentieth-century Taoist philosopher Wei Wu Wei quipped, "Why are you unhappy? Because 99 percent of everything you think, and of everything you do, is for yourself—and there isn't one."

The gravitational metaphor takes on more weight when the sun is replaced by a black hole, and orbital processes are replaced by phenomena that just suck. In other words, all the contractions we're discussing add up to create so much weight that *everything* gets sucked in to feed one massive me, like a super-massive black hole. Narcissism is a matter of degree. Insatiable consumerism is just one iteration of this sucking process, which breeds every form of the modern epidemic of excess consumption. I like to suck in thoughts and ideas as much as someone else likes to suck in burgers and fries.

As we shed this weight on the journey to lighten up, we'll drop tons of contractions, and our narrative will change from "What's in it for me?" to "How can I help?" We'll find ourselves spending more time on the openness side of the pulsation and less time on the closure side. Instead of taking, we'll give. Instead of grasping, we'll offer. In the terms of Abraham Maslow's hierarchy of needs, we'll replace deficiency needs with abundance needs. To reach this level of en*light*enment, we need to replace the long-standing habit of sucking up to ourselves with a fresh habit of offering ourselves.

The point for now is that contraction is not a static affair. The deepest levels of contraction have been around for so long that they can feel monolithic and impenetrable, which manifests in the feeling that we can't change. We feel stuck in unhealthy grooves that have been cut every time we capitulated to compulsive thinking or repetitive behavior. We feel these grooves as our habits and addictions. But contraction is dynamic: we can alter the flow of things. Nothing is as solid as it seems. (Just ask any physicist.) Even the densest thing in the world—the primordial contraction of the adamantine ego—can be accessed, opened, and released.

CONTEMPLATION

Sit in silence for a few minutes. Then see if you can *feel* the pulsation of your awareness: as it expands to make contact with the present moment and then immediately contracts to generate commentary about that contact. This exposes a secondary level of contraction, but it's a good start. With some practice, see if you can then feel into the primordial contraction, which manifests as the usually unconscious feeling that *I* am having that commentary; *I* am experiencing this. Because this contraction is so subtle, you might not be able to touch into it just yet. For now, try to feel into the active process, the alternating current, of opening and then immediately contracting. Don't worry if you can't feel it; just slowing down to try is revelatory. The practices in part 2 of this book, especially the practices of open awareness, will help.

The fact that many people can't initially feel this alternating current is diagnostic. For most, it doesn't feel like an alternating current, but instead it's more like a closed direct current where everything is directed to *me*. Even this "failure" is a success, because it shows us where we're stuck and how self-referential we are. It reveals the degree of our contraction.

Even though openness is the natural state, because we're so contracted, it initially feels like opening is artificial. But that's only because we've been so contracted for so long.

STRATIFIED

Another characteristic of contraction is that it is not a monolithic phenomenon. The sedimentation of our contractions has been accumulating from beginningless time, so it's layers upon layers—all the way up and down, generating a spectrum from subtle to gross, temporary to almost permanent, individual to collective, and conscious to totally unconscious. The antidote here is to simply acknowledge and appreciate the depth and variety of our contractive ways, and the manner in which they collectively conspire to keep us away from the truth.

CONTEMPLATION

Touch back into the forceful super contractors we discussed in chapter 4, like anger, fear, or intense self-consciousness. Feel into the intensity of these massive general contractors. Now take a minute to touch into less forceful but omnipresent contractors, like irritation, impatience, or frustration. Then feel into even more subtle levels, like occasional moments of touchiness or incredulity. Finally, touch into the very subtle levels, like getting distracted, or the sense of "me." After you do this exercise, drop the whole thing, and relax. Notice how the contractions reverberate. Like a big rock thrown into a still pond, it takes a few minutes for the splash to dissipate.

AUTOMATIC

Contractions also have the characteristic of being automatic—preprogrammed, and involuntary, like the "I can't help myself!" reactivity discussed earlier. Something arises and you automatically contract. Sometimes it's a healthy biological reflex, like the instinctive reaction to a driver cutting you off. Often, it's an unhealthy contraction, like the pouting that occurs when someone criticizes you. Threats to your beliefs and opinions can stimulate contractions that are just as reflexive as menaces to your life.

The automatic and involuntary nature of contraction is a central concept in reverse meditation, because *to deautomatize is to deconstruct.* In other words, contractions do not have to be automatic, and suffering does not have to result from pain. Because contractions are often preprogrammed, they can be deprogrammed. If something activates the preset button, you can learn how to hit the reset button. That's the remedy, and that's the gift of meditation.

CONTEMPLATION

In your day-to-day life, start noticing how automatically you contract when encountering offensive words, like FUCK YOU! If that doesn't do it, come up with the most offensive words you can think of, and shout them out to yourself while looking in a mirror. Do you feel the contraction, like a gut punch? Words are just harmless sound waves, what Edward Conze calls the "initial datum." But we render the pure impure by superimposing all our baggage onto that sound. To get a sense of how deautomatization works, repeat an offensive word over and over to yourself for a few minutes. Notice how it gradually loses meaning as you strip the word back to harmless sound.

Meditation works in a similar way. By observing the contents of your mind over and over, those contents lose their power. You may even realize, as did the psychologist William James, that "a great many people think they are thinking when they are merely rearranging their prejudices." It's just the same underlying story, centered around me, repurposed over and over. We automate storylines that we keep telling ourselves to preserve the narrative of ego, but those storylines lose their pop when we ask ourselves to listen to them for the thousandth time.

INSTANTANEOUS

Automaticity leads directly to the next characteristic of contraction: its lightning-fast speed. It's so fast that contraction seems to arise simultaneously with perception. As we'll see later in the practice of open awareness, any perception that solidifies the sense of self and other *is* a contraction. If you've ever been close to a lightning strike, the flash of light and the thunderclap seem to happen at exactly the same time. Flash/bang! But what's really happening is that lightning raises the temperature of the surrounding air to some fifty thousand degrees. The super-heated air rapidly expands, then creates a deafening shock wave as it contracts, slapping molecules into each other at thunderous velocities. The flash of lightning precedes the clap of thunder even when they seem simultaneous.

Expansion and contraction occur at similar lightning speeds: the pulsation occurs with such velocity that we no longer see it as an alternating current. It's like looking at your light bulb and seeing a continuous glow, forgetting that the current is actually alternating back and forth fifty to sixty times per second.

To point out this speed, let's return to the idea of words being harmless soundwaves. When you hear a word, you instantly derive meaning from it. But meaning is not inherent in the sensory experience. Meaning is a secondary imposition. The initial datum is mere compression and rarefaction waves that we perceive as sound, which we further recognize as a word, and which we then burden with all our associations triggered by that word. In a similar vein, try looking at a heap of hundred-dollar US bills without reacting in a desirous way. Most of us immediately bring a mountain of meaning to what is just a stack of paper.

Here's a more revelatory example. According to neuroscience and Buddhist psychology, you can't register sight and sound (or feel and touch, taste and feel, or any other combination of the senses) at the same time. Sensory data is registered by consciousness serially, not simultaneously. It's only the speed of flickering from one sense faculty to the next that creates the illusion of simultaneity.

CONTEMPLATION

Turn on the TV or radio and try listening to your native language as if it were a foreign language. It's almost impossible. The imputation of meaning happens so fast that it's extremely difficult to separate out the meaning from the sound. But you can get a sense of this deconstruction by taking any word and repeating it over and over. Say the word "dog" a hundred times, and watch the dog shed the meaning we bring to it.

I rented a moving truck recently, and above the speedometer was a decal that cautioned SPEED KILLS—SLOW DOWN AND LIVE. In a similar vein, the velocity of our contractions kills the authentic experience of life. Among the ancient meditative texts from the East that reflect on the speed of "mind-moments" (in Buddhism called *dharmas*, or atoms of experience), one is the great Buddhist encyclopedia known as the *Treasury of Abhidharma*, which states, "There are sixty-five instants in the time it takes a healthy man to snap his fingers." In the modern West, scientists—using strobe lights called *tachistoscopes*—discovered that two successive lights flashed within 100-250 milliseconds (a thousand milliseconds equals one second) were seen as continuous by an untrained observer. The philosopher Evan Thompson writes:

> Scientists often use the metaphor of the "spotlight" to describe how your attention can move around your field of vision and focus selectively on certain areas, so that you can detect more efficiently what falls within the spotlight. Although this metaphor suggests that sustaining your attention at a location is like continuously shining a light there, recent studies have found that the way sustained attention enhances perception is discrete and periodic, as if the spotlight blinks on and off every 100-150 milliseconds like a strobe light.[11]

A trained mind, however, can detect the discontinuity between flashes of light ten times faster—at ten to twenty milliseconds—than the mind of an observer who sees the flashes as continuous. The "stream of consciousness" (a phrase coined by William James) is only an unbroken stream to the untrained mind. To the trained mind, it's more like the "staccato of consciousness," or discrete clips of mind moments that are con-fused together, creating the illusion of a stream, a process that scientists call "flicker fusion."

The meditation practices at the beginning of part 2 are designed to slow the mind down to the point where that confusion comes apart, and you can detect the alternating current of expansion and contraction. It's not just "slow down and live"—with meditation it's *slow down and see*. We need space to see things. The reason we don't see the inside of our eyelids, for example, is because there's no space between our eyes and the lid. Meditation allows you to perceive the gap between stimulus and response, between the initial perception and your reaction/contraction to it, and in that space you have a choice: to contract or stay open, to react or respond (and at the deepest level: to be or not to be).

All the meditations in Buddhism can be classified as either shamatha ("tranquility, quiescence") practices or vipashyana ("insight") practices.

Shamatha, a practice of "peaceful abiding," puts the brakes on things; vipashyana allows us to see into them. These meditations are the antidotes to the automatic nature of our contractions—to our suffering—and they facilitate the process of deautomatization. By slowing down, we allow the mind to relax and open. Thoughts start to delink (deautomatize), like uncoupling the cars in a long train, and we begin to see the space between them. Putting the brakes on the mind reveals the breaks in the mind, and freedom lies in those breaks.

To deconstruct is to deautomatize, and to deautomatize is to decelerate. Things only appear to happen automatically because they happen so quickly. When we sit in meditation, and physically boycott movement, we're also boycotting the furious movement of the mind. Instead of racing along the interstate of life, we pull over to the rest stop and savor the view.

CONTEMPLATION

Take some time to think more about the nature of words and the responses we feel when we hear one. In addition to the instantaneous imputation of meaning onto the word, we add yet another lightning-fast process that generates the illusion that "I" am hearing the word. There appears to be an object, the sound out there, and a perceiving subject, me in here. But that's an illusion. Duality is illusory. We have to really slow down and look, but there is no "you" hearing the sound. There is no subject perceiving an object. The practice of open awareness will guide us into this realization, and later chapters will elaborate. For now, take my word on it: *you* are not hearing that sound.

HABITUAL AND IMPULSIVE

The automaticity of our contractions suggests their instinctive, reflexive, and habitual nature. Tap a rubber hammer below your kneecap, and your foot reflexively springs up. See something you don't like, and watch yourself reflexively contract. Every time we contract, we're reinforcing a pattern that just becomes stronger, more reflexive, and increasingly habitual. Whether we know it or not, we're always becoming increasingly familiar with contraction. That's why we're so good at it. We've practiced contraction so often, and for so long, that we're now in performance mode.

Because we unwittingly practice contraction all the time, we're completely habituated to the closure it represents. We're in a groove we continue to cut. We don't even have to think about it. Contraction thinks for us. Contraction "does" us. It operates at the level of instinct. Whenever we feel threatened, at biological, psychological, ideological, or spiritual levels, we close down like a Venus flytrap on steroids. Someone challenges our beliefs and we contract; something offends us and we contract; something violates our space and we contract.

Meditation is essentially the practice of reversing this impulse and habituating to openness. It offers a direct antidote to all the ways we put the squeeze on ourselves.

CONTEMPLATION

For the next week, notice how often you act out of mindless impulse. You get a little bored and impulsively check your phone, habitually grab a bag of chips, or instinctively turn on the TV. When those urges arise, feel into the contraction that accompanies them. When the itch occurs to do something, notice the contraction that scratches it.

When you feel the urge to grab your phone, or reply to that text, or mindlessly open the fridge, pause for a second, and touch into how addicted you are to your contractive impulses. Because ego is the archetype of contraction and is reinforced with secondary contractions, you can feel the pulse of these pinches with every impulse to move.

Contractions are not only the result of our habits; they are the genesis of habit formation. Even though many of them are unhealthy, we're addicted to them. They "fix" the ego, so we crave them. This addiction is usually concealed in the relentless activity of daily life, but it becomes painfully evident when movement is taken away, as in sitting meditation. Let's turn to the meditations that allow us to get a feel for them and that show us how to release them.

PART 2

THE FORMAL MEDITATIONS

CHAPTER 7

REFERENTIAL MEDITATION

Form-Based Practice

We can all come to see the hardships of life, illness,
and injury as stepping-stones on which our souls can
grow and ascend toward that oneness with the Divine.
It is through how we deal with such challenges, by
recovering our sense of divinity and connectedness, that
determines their ability to empower our growth.

—EBEN ALEXANDER

What gives light must endure burning.

—VICTOR FRANKL

The term "meditation" encompasses many forms of contemplative practice. Our exploration of formal meditations begins with instruction in referential, or form-based, practices—practices that refer the distracted mind back to some form, or referent (like the breath, a candle, a mantra, or any other anchor), to help the meditation stay on track. Referential meditations such as the one introduced in this chapter serve as useful training wheels.

In subsequent chapters, once you've found your balance, you will drop the training wheels and ride freely into nonreferential, or formless, practices. For now, however, in the instructions for sitting meditation that follow, the referents will be the body and breath. The intention will be to stay mindful of the body and breath as a way to become more attuned to the present moment.

When it comes to discovering the right view of sacredness, referential meditations serve as an actual practice of wholeness, or holy-ness. Sitting down creates a useful contrast medium; the stasis of sitting allows us to better see the relentless movement of the mind and thereby discover how "partial" and profane we usually are with our awareness. The "continuous partial attention" of the untrained mind is like radio static that prevents us from tuning in to the sacred.

The most subtle and constant form of profanity is also one of the most immediate and ubiquitous instances of contraction—our impulse to distract, or pull apart, from the present moment. Once this first-order pulling apart from the sanctity of the present moment occurs, we immediately cascade into further levels of contraction, pulling ourselves further and further away from reality by getting lost in conceptual ("contractual") proliferation. Our minds are so good at distraction that we even get distracted from our distractions. No wonder we feel that something is missing! Direct contact with reality is missing, buried under layers of distraction/contraction.

Along with serving to bring sacred attention to wholeness, referential meditations also act as a gesture of respect, as a kind of bow or genuflection to the present moment, which sanctifies your relationship to whatever the present moment holds. With the reverse meditations, you'll work to establish a sacred relationship to the types of unwanted experience that you deem the most sacrilegious—for instance, pain. Reverse meditations require reframing your relationship to unwanted experience, and "taking a bow" to your experience of the present moment is the first step in that reframing. The referential meditations therefore double as reverential meditations, by nurturing a reverence to whatever arises.

Before I enter my shrine room at home, or enter a temple in Asia, I pause at the doorway, gather myself, and bow. In a 2020 essay about what makes a space sacred, Vanessa Zuisei Goddard describes the significance of such reverential gestures:

> It's a way to align the body, gather the mind, and say, "I am here. I am aware, and I am preparing to do something different [the *reverse*] from what I did before." I am deliberately, wakefully turning toward what is whole because that's the reality I want to create. Entering a sacred space reminds us there is holiness here, and if we move too fast, talk too loud, we'll miss it. We need space and time to look and listen and feel the real. Bustle and busyness are the enemies of heirophany. There is no better way to keep the experience of the sacred at bay than to rush from one task to the next. Instead, entering the sacred requires a drastic slowing down.[1]

That drastic slowing down is a central aspect of sitting meditation. By simply sitting down you're going on strike against all the "bustle and busyness" that stand in conflict with manifestations of the sacred. You're boycotting the speed of your restless mind, by engaging in a "sit-in" that also opens you to the experience of the sacred.

In the rest of this chapter, we'll unfold sitting meditation in three phases: body, breath, and mind. The practice here builds on itself in a linear way—but each phase also supports the other phases in a tri-directional way: what you do with your body affects your mind and breath; what you do with your mind affects your body and breath; what you do with your breath affects your body and mind. The three phases generate a stable tripod, with each phase leaning on and propping up the other two.

BODY PHASE

The first phase of sitting meditation establishes the ground and engages the wisdom of the body. Milarepa said, "Having discovered a sanctuary within my body . . . I had no need for a monastery." Trungpa Rinpoche taught, "Just by taking the proper posture, sooner or later you will find yourself meditating." You are creating a sacred space, which facilitates the recognition that the body exists only in the present moment and that our senses operate only in the present. We literally can't see the future, hear the past, smell the future, or touch and taste the past. So the first phase uses your senses to "bring you to your senses." Phase 1 entrains the discursive mind—the monkey mind, which constantly flits between past and future—locking it into the body that is always already present.

Even though the body is your focus in the first phase, you'll start phase 1 with an attitude, or "mental posture," that supports the body. The body phase begins by taking your seat with an uplifted, dignified, and even regal attitude. It's a posture of confidence and nobility. You're assuming your throne in this world, and you're about to rule the kingdom of your own mind.

✺INSTRUCTION

If you're sitting on a meditation cushion, start by feeling your connection to the earth. If you're sitting on a chair, plant your feet squarely on the ground, and pull yourself forward on the chair so your back is away from the support. Your body is your personal earth, and you're reestablishing its connection to the literal earth. Place your hands on your thighs, not too far forward (which might pull you forward) or too close (which could push you back). This "middle way" approach is a maxim that runs throughout the meditative journey.

Sit with a spine that is firm but not stiff. The posture is disciplined but not militaristic. This usually means pulling the shoulders up and back to straighten out the spine, which invites a masculine quality of strength, immutability, and fearlessness. This posture of the back is tempered and balanced with a soft and receptive front, which invites a more feminine quality of accommodation, openness, and gentleness.

The two qualities of fearlessness and gentleness in your physical posture will be extended into your relationship with the contents of your mind—inviting a fearless yet gentle relationship to whatever arises. That is, your physical posture nurtures the mental posture you want to take.

The central axis of instruction is to open and expose your heart. In ancient Sanskrit and Pali texts, the same word (*chitta, citta*) is used for both "mind" and "heart"—in the Buddhist tradition, "mind" is more accurately understood as "heart-mind." This aligns with my favorite definition of meditation, as "habituation to openness," and it anticipates how you'll use the practice of openness as an antidote to contraction.

By pulling your shoulders back and opening your heart, you're encouraging an opening of the mind. With gentleness and fearlessness, you're going to expose yourself to yourself and discover who you really are. Then you're going to open yourself further to others. Every aspect of the posture hinges on this axial instruction. Open your heart center, and then watch every other facet of the practice align itself around this central point.

INSTRUCTION (CONTINUED)

To flesh out this posture fully, next bring your head into alignment with your heart by centering your head on top of your spinal column. For many of us, this means pulling our heads back. This aspect of posture reins the head back in, placing it in harmony with the heart.

Many people "head" into the world with their thinking. I am one of those people, and I work to keep my intellect in resonance with my intuition. I tend to hunch over, think too much, and lead with my head, not my heart. This collapsed posture is also my character armor, an unconscious way I keep myself from being too open and vulnerable. "Good head and shoulders" is common parlance in the meditation world, and one I strive to remember.

INSTRUCTION (CONTINUED)

You can sit with your eyes open or closed. I was trained to practice with my eyes open, which is slightly more advanced, but it's also more conducive to mixing meditation with post-meditation. Unless you're blind, you don't move through the world with your eyes closed. Meditating with your eyes open allows you to more easily bring the meditative mind with you into the world. If you wish to practice with your eyes open, keep your gaze down, about six feet or so in front of you, with your visual field open and relaxed. This invites an opening of the mind's eye, a receptive mental field that can accommodate anything.

With this said, I sometimes start my meditations with my eyes briefly closed. This helps me gather my mind, and it invites more direct contact with my body. After a few minutes, I'll open my eyes and keep my gaze down. See what works for you. As final refinements, place your tongue on the back of your upper teeth, which decreases salivary flow; and part your lips slightly, as if you're whispering "ahhh."

BREATH PHASE

Breath is like a bridge between body and mind, a link between phase 1 and phase 3 of our sitting meditation. The lungs are also a bridge between the inside of the body and the outside. Where exactly does air become breath, and breath become air? When does that breath turn into you? Are you really different from the space around you? These questions will take on new meaning in the next chapter when we explore the practice of open awareness. The breath is one thing that can operate both consciously and unconsciously, thereby serving as the bridge between the conscious and unconscious mind. Relating to the breath properly also acts as a channel between duality (body/mind, inside/outside) and nonduality. Breathing incorporates some of the body's form (you can still feel it) and some of the mind's formlessness (but you can't really touch it). Breath is of such importance that even the Latin *spiritus*, which brings us the word "spirit," derives from the word "breath."

INSTRUCTION

As you sit, simply bring your attention to the natural movement of your breath. Don't imagine it; don't visualize it. Feel it; be it. Let your mind "ride" the movement of your breath.

"The attitude towards breathing in meditation is to become the breathing. Try to identify completely rather than watching it. You are the breath; the breath is you. Breath is coming out of your nostrils, going out and dissolving into the atmosphere, into the space," says Trungpa Rinpoche. "Just boycott your breath; boycott your concentration on the breath. As your breath goes out, let it dissolve." His advice for meditating on the breath focuses on out-breathing: "in-breathing is just space," he says.

> One does breathe in, but that's not a big deal . . . So it's out, dissolve, gap; out, dissolve, gap. It is constant opening, gap, abandoning, boycotting. Boycotting in this case is a significant word. If you hold onto your breath, you are holding onto yourself constantly. Once you begin to boycott the end of the outbreath, then there's no world left, except that the next outbreath reminds you to tune in. So you tune in, dissolve, tune in, dissolve, tune in, dissolve.[2]

Phase 2 can also double as an appreciation practice. Appreciate the fact that you're still breathing, and therefore alive. You're so close to death: you only have to breathe out, don't breathe in, and you're dead. You are literally one breath away from death. Appreciate every breath as if it could be your last.

With these two phases, you're simply sitting and breathing. That's it. The profundity of sitting meditation comes from its simplicity. Don't try to outsmart the practice. Surrender to it; let it defeat you. The modern complex mind doesn't stand a chance against simplicity. Let this practice take you down— into the wisdom of your body and breath—and therefore into the present moment.

MIND PHASE

The body and breath phases create a background of silence and stillness that allows us to better see the movement of the mind. We're usually so active in our busy lives that we don't see the mind's relentless activity. Our incessant physical movement acts as camouflage that masks the movement of our mind. By sitting still, we remove the camouflage, and mental activity stands out.

🌿 INSTRUCTION

The instruction for the mind phase is simple: whenever anything distracts you from your body or breath, mentally say to yourself "thinking," and return to body and breath. It's gentle yet precise, like popping a bubble with a feather.

"Thinking" is not a reprimand. It's merely an act of recognition that your mind has strayed. You're not hammering your thoughts into submission. Thoughts (the term refers to any contents of mind, such as emotion, fantasy, or imagination) are never a problem. Left alone, they dissolve, like campfire sparks vanishing harmlessly into the nighttime sky.

Many people struggle with meditation because they develop an adversarial relationship to their thoughts. They think that meditation means stopping their thoughts, or somehow wrestling them down. The problem is not with thoughts, but with our inappropriate relationship to thoughts. Not leaving them alone. Whenever we grasp after thoughts or push them away—both of which require some level of contraction—we're relating inappropriately. Every time we label our thoughts as "thinking," and return to body and breath, we're acknowledging a subtle level of contraction, releasing our grip, and conserving energy.

Using the label "thinking" does not muzzle the mind. "Thinking" quiets the ceaseless commentary that inevitably accompanies the arising of thought. That's the noise.

INSTRUCTION (CONTINUED)

Every thought that arises is "clickbait," ready to seduce you into its content. When a thought pops up, let it arise. Just don't click on it. Don't buy into it.[3] Stay with your body and breath. "Double click" on that experience, which doesn't open into anything but the present moment. And when you label your thoughts "thinking," do so lovingly.

> Thoughts are the children of your mind. Unless you're deranged, you don't abuse your children. You love them. You have space for them, no matter how unruly they sometimes appear. You hold them when they throw a tantrum; you accommodate their play; you have patience for their challenging behavior. The underlying theme of the mind phase of instruction is to love your mind.

The meditative maxim "not too tight, not too loose" comes into play with the three phases of this practice. Some effort is involved, but not in excess: the posture is firm, but not stiff; your attitude is serious, but also playful; it takes discipline, but not too much. In terms of duration, the "middle way" means practicing not too long and not too short. Twenty minutes is great, but if you can only do ten, that's fine. Mornings are always good, but anytime works. The Zen master Yasutani warns, "You will never succeed if you do *zazen* [meditation] only when you have a whim to, and give up easily. You must carry on steadfastly."[4] (This advice will be important as you progress into the reverse meditations, because it's so easy to give up practice when things start to hurt. You will learn to reverse this default and to use the hurt to *start* your meditation.)

PRAPAÑCA

Sitting meditation is a way to develop an open meditative mind, in which a spark of thought arises and harmlessly dissolves into the space of the mind. In the contracted non-meditative mind, by contrast, that same spark arises but then lands in a vat of gasoline: "Whoosh!" Off we go into a fiery fantasy. This reaction is what we've been calling *conceptual proliferation—prapañca* (pronounced pra-phan-cha) in Sanskrit—and it refers to the insatiable tendency of the small mind to put a spin on whatever happens. Something pops up, and like a hungry journalist looking for a story, conceptual proliferation runs with it.

Prapañca takes simple sensory stimulation and weaves it into complex storylines, creating the narratives that script the comedies, tragedies, and dramas of our lives. This is pollution at its cognitive core, the unsustainable mental activity that consumes tremendous energy. Thought commenting on thought, contraction poured on top of contraction. Prapañca is exposed with every meditation we'll explore, but it will become explosively important later when we turn to the reverse meditations. Conceptual proliferation is what transforms intense sensory stimulation, or pain, into suffering. The adjective "intense" is already prapañca at work: if left alone, pain is just sensory stimulation. Like contraction itself, prapañca is everywhere, because prapañca is a mental manifestation of contraction.

Prapañca is an aspect of the egoic mind, because ego itself is just a contracted storyline. Ego lives on conceptual proliferation, authoring its very existence through prapañca. But by working with conceptual proliferation in meditation, you can release egoic contraction from your life, one storyline at a time.

OUTER, INNER, AND SECRET SILENCE

In the mind phase of sitting meditation, the objective was to recognize and quiet the endless commentary that accompanies the arising of thought. The reverse meditations deal with intense or "loud" experiences, so to enter the "volume levels" of the reverse meditations fully prepared, you'll need to expand your understanding of silence. Outer silence is obvious: just turn down the volume "out there." By learning how to be quiet inside, however, you can enter the noise outside, and bring silence along with you. Inner silence is about turning down the volume "in here"—or about silencing our protest against the way things are. The acoustic ecologist Gordon Hempton has suggested that real quiet is not an absence of sound but an absence of noise. This brings to mind a story about the Thai master Ajahn Chah, who was leading a meditation intensive during which monks had to wake up at 3:00 am to begin their practice. Villagers nearby were celebrating a festival at the same time, with revelry going till dawn. After several intolerable days, a young monk came to Ajahn Chah complaining that he couldn't meditate with all the noise. The master told him, "The noise isn't bothering you. You are bothering the noise." (The Indian master Shantideva taught a similar lesson, famously saying, "You can try to pave the world with leather, or you can wear shoes.") Inner silence is putting a muffler on your reactive mind.[5]

Inner silence also works with silencing the eyes. Pay attention to how you look at things, and notice how you skid across appearances at the speed of sight, skimming just what you need to make cheap sense out of your visual world. Usually, our eyes move as rapidly as our mind, glancing across the surface of things like a stone skipping on top of water. We rarely slow down and sink into the depths of what we perceive. When I'm in conversation with someone, and my gaze is not set on that person, I'm not fully attending to them. I'm often formulating my response before they're even done talking, hearing but not really listening. How often do we look but not really see?

CONTEMPLATION

Set this book down, and look directly ahead at whatever is in front of you for a minute. Notice the propensity of your eyes to dart around. If they do, bring your eyes back to the object. Notice how holding your eyes steadily onto an object serves to also steady the mind, a form of "eye shamatha," so to speak. When I'm at the gym and catching my breath from some reps on the curling machine, instead of looking around the gym, I rest my gaze on whatever is in front of me. If I'm doing this eye-meditation in more formal sessions, instead of just at the gym (or wherever), I'll pulsate my awareness, alternating from a more intensive focus to an open gaze in order to curtail my usual visual distractedness. The idea is to keep the gaze from becoming discursive, even when it is relaxed. As with many of our meditations, this practice is simultaneously diagnostic and prescriptive. It helps you become aware of how visually discursive you are, and it guides you toward what you need to do to perceive things more deeply.

By holding our gaze on things, we can penetrate into their true nature. Never do we look away so quickly as when we're in pain (or when we avert our eyes from seeing others in pain), and therefore we don't allow ourselves the opportunity to see through it. Reverse meditation is a practice that helps us reverse this discursive gaze, engage in a meditative stare-down, and cultivate a kind of X-ray vision that allows us to penetrate pain, seeing it for what it really is.[6]

Secret silence goes one step further, and it will be brought to fruition with the reverse meditations. With some practice in outer and inner silence, you can learn how to find silence *in* the noise, stillness *in* the movement, the bliss *in* the pain. Goddard writes:

I've watched scores of newcomers grow hushed as they enter the hallway that leads to our zendo. Many of them have never been to a monastery, know nothing about Zen or Buddhism, and aren't even necessarily interested in meditation. Yet invariably, the moment they enter the space, something happens. Regardless of whether they feel drawn or repelled, their initial response is what you'd expect from someone who is suddenly, starkly confronted with reality: silence.

Silence is both a necessary ingredient for the experience of heirophany and a common response to it. We need to be willing to relinquish our incessant dialogue in order to experience the sacred. A busy mind or tongue generates static, effectively preventing us from attuning ourselves to the holy . . . in order to be in relationship with the sacred, we must be willing to become still and quiet.[7]

The sacred stops us in our tracks (the stillness of phase 1), silences the busy tongue (phase 2), and hushes the hectic mind (phase 3). But this is a bidirectional phenomenon—you can get to the sacred in a more unconditional way. The experience of heirophany, of manifesting sacred space, silences body, speech, and mind. But conversely, by silencing body, speech, and mind through meditation, you can experience heirophany here and now. You can enter the monastery of the moment through the mindfulness developed in the practice of referential meditation. "Let this sacred silence bring you back to yourself, back to the realm of the real," says Goddard. She continues:

In the sacred space that is our bodymind we practice noble silence with the intent to abide in reality. Again, not because at other times our living isn't real but because we forget that it is. We get lost in our heads, in each other, in our work, *in those things that will buffer us from the pain* of being lost or simply the pain of living. We therefore need spaces and objects and practices to remind us that since our center is everywhere and our circumference nowhere, it's not possible for us to get lost. We need deep, abiding silence to remember that no matter how far we think we've strayed, how long we've wandered, we've never really left home.[8]

Paradoxically, by bringing the mind to the point of the present moment, you open that moment up. Referential shamatha will reveal to you just how often you contract at the mind level. Every time you get lost in thought, you're contracting after that thought. Pay attention to your mind and you'll see how it happens *all* the time.

The sitting meditation explored in this chapter, and the practice of open awareness we'll be discussing in the next two chapters, all pave the way into the reverse meditations that are the destination of our journey. You don't need to master these preliminary practices in order to move on to reverse meditation, but they help set the stage.

CHAPTER 8

NONREFERENTIAL MEDITATION

An Introduction to Open Awareness

Let your mind come forth without fixating it anywhere.

—THE DIAMOND SUTRA

If you go toward the suffering and allow yourself
to go through it, you discover suffering is
joy. It's a little itch on the edge of bliss.

—ROBERT THURMAN

Progressing from the practice of referential meditation into the
sphere of nonreferential practice represents a subtle but major step
forward in the journey of meditation. The hitching post of a referential
practice is an aid for tethering and taming the mind, but at a certain
point the post holds you back. In the next two chapters, you'll be
learning about nonreferential meditations that go beyond sitting in
mindfulness, and expand your meditation to embrace the entirety of
your life, including everything that hurts.

Buddhists sometimes refer to nonreferential meditations as *objectless shamatha* or *shamatha without a sign*. Other meditators call it *nonreferential mindfulness, awareness of awareness*, or *formless meditation*. Scientists use the term "open monitoring." I prefer *open awareness*, because that framing is resonant with the definition of meditation as "habituation to openness." Instead of constantly closing down and habituating to contraction, open awareness allows us to reverse that habit and default into opening up.[1]

Open awareness is a multivalent practice with many applications and levels. I've been doing it for decades, and the more I do it, the more I discover. Depending on your interests, you can keep the practice at entry levels and derive great benefit, or you can go to the deep end of the pool and plunge into the nature of mind and reality. For our purposes, entry-level benefits are enough. But I will point out some of the deeper aspects of open awareness so you can appreciate the profundity of this practice. As the material progresses into these depths, don't worry if it doesn't speak to you. Skim or skip as you like.

Whether you know it or not, you're familiar with closed and con-tracted states of mind, because you "meditate" on them all the time. Every time you grasp, or get distracted, you're practicing contraction. A practice of openness can therefore feel unfamiliar at first, or even intimidating. But because openness is actually the natural state, it becomes easier as you repeatedly return to your nature.

If contraction is the source of your suffering, openness is the key to your liberation. And as with contraction, openness is something you can feel. It's expansive, receptive, and refreshing. Importantly, this somatic component allows you to use your felt sense of contraction as a new prompt to open. Once you sensitize yourself to your contractions, every time you feel them, you can reverse that tendency by opening. Obstacle transforms into opportunity.

Claiming that contraction is something you can feel implies that you can feel all our contractions. This is a partial truth. If the contraction is very subtle, or constant, you lose touch with it. It's like an air condition-ing system that's always been on and suddenly turns off. Until it stopped, you had no idea it was even on. Openness, like contraction, comes in degrees. From here till the end of our journey, we'll start exploring the practice of open awareness by working with more overt forms of contraction, and gradually work our way down to covert levels. Layer by layer—contraction upon contraction—through open awareness we'll work our way down to . . . *nothing*!

MUCH ADO ABOUT NOTHING

The development of open awareness ultimately reveals that the primordial contraction—that subtle cramp at the deepest levels of the unconscious body-mind, which generates our sense of self—is fundamentally grasping *onto* nothing (and all the secondary contractions are grasping *after* nothing). Pause for a moment here, and try to make contact with the primordial cramp: What does this contraction actually feel like? It feels like *me*. This contraction is so constant, and so subtle, that we've come to identify with it as our very sense of self. The untamed mind is like a clenched fist. We have to pry our fingers open one at a time, relaxing a fist we didn't even know we had clenched. So don't worry if you can't feel it yet.

And that fist is clenched around . . . what? Picture a whirlpool once again—and consider that at the center of a powerful whirlpool is nothing. You won't discern the void in the flowing whirlpools of a stream, but empty your bathtub to get a glimpse as the water goes down the drain, and you'll be looking at a centerless whirlpool. In a similar way, the primordial contraction is contracting onto formless, empty awareness, a *contraction that actually generates the illusion that there is something*. This contraction/grasping generates the sense of self, and by immediate implication, the sense of other (you can't have one without the other). It's a grasping that generates the illusion of inside and outside, of duality, and therefore generates all our suffering. It may not be your direct experience yet, but the practice of open awareness, which culminates in nondual experiences, will show you that you suffer at the most fundamental levels every time you fracture the world into self and other, generating duality.

The more refined aspects of the practice of open awareness, which allow us to make contact with the primordial contraction, bring previously unconscious processes into the light of consciousness.[2] Now we're getting down to it. Now we're unearthing contractions so nuanced they fly below the radar of the conscious mind. Here lies the true brilliance of open awareness. In order to spiritually wake up, all the forces of the dark side, buried deep in the unconscious mind, must be brought to light.[3] Otherwise, they continue to exert their massive backstage influence on our onstage lives, and we continue to stumble around in the dark.

The practice of open awareness allows us to touch into layers of contractions all the way from the gross to the most subtle. The subtle contractions are the true super contractors, because they're so omnipresent and generative: subtle does not mean ineffectual. The subtle effects, fashions, and propagates the gross, and the contrast medium of open awareness allows us to identify every contraction along the spectrum. Just as the contrast medium of resting in stillness through sitting meditation (referential shamatha) exposes movement, the practice of inviting the mind to rest in open awareness exposes how constantly our mind closes.

In other words, by doing something (opening up) that's the *reverse* of what we usually do (closing down), we see things never seen before. So, on one level, both sitting meditation and the practice of open awareness double as a type of reverse meditation. Sitting still is the reverse of what we usually do in our busy lives; opening up is the reverse of our habitually contractive ways. The formal reverse meditations will take this retro narrative to the summit.

The revelations of open awareness are sometimes bittersweet. They expose a conflict of interest that helps you understand unconscious resistance to this practice. The more evolved (trans-egoic) aspects of your identity want to open; the less evolved aspects (ego) prefer to stay closed. Understanding the full spectrum of your identity allows you to relate to some of the opposition that might arise when doing this practice.

MIND SPACE

Our journey deals with the maturation of meditation—expanding it to develop an industrial-strength mind that can handle anything. This doesn't mean a muscular mind that can withstand the blows of life like an Olympic boxer. It means cultivating a mind that is the reverse of our normal sense of toughness.

Open awareness meditation offers a way to nurture the mind's ability to handle anything by means of learning to mix your mind with space— the epitome of openness and indestructibility. Outer space is not the same as the inner space of the mind, but neither is it different. You can therefore learn about the inner space you want to cultivate by exploring its outer analog. Space possesses a number of unique characteristics. On the one hand, it's the softest thing in the world. Move your hand back and forth through space and feel how soft it is. There is nothing softer than space. On the other hand, there is nothing more indestructible. Pick up a knife and try to cut it. Light a match and try to burn it. Nothing can hurt space. So, it's also the toughest thing in the universe. You're going to develop an indestructible quality of mind using the softest thing in the world.

Space can accommodate everything without being adversely affected by anything. It is the holding environment for the entire universe, and it can easily hold your pain. Space is also the lightest thing in the universe. Pick it up. There's nothing lighter than space. It's the definition of unfettered and free, utterly unburdened and boundless. Finally, space is groundless and ungraspable. Nothing can land on space. You can never get a grip on it, possess it, claim it, or appropriate it. You can't put a sticky note on space.

Nondual traditions use outer elements, like space, to invoke inner qualities. In Dzogchen, sky gazing is a formal meditation where the student gazes into space to invite an open mind. Clouds float through space like thoughts float through the mind. Blizzards, hurricanes, lightning, hail, and endless weather patterns course through space, which accommodates it all and remains unfazed by it all. In the *Sadhana of Mahāmudrā*, Trungpa Rinpoche wrote, "Good and bad, happy and sad, all thoughts vanish into emptiness like the imprint of a bird in the sky." The sky can teach us. The Tibetan tradition engages "nature dharma" (*ri-cho*), and "symbolic guru," where nature becomes your natural teacher, and the guru is found in the elements of reality. Milarepa said, "Phenomena are all the books one needs."

Imagine a mind that is loving, kind, generous, and compassionate. This is the softness of a spacious mind. When you open your heart and mind, everything touches you. Imagine a mind that is immovable, impenetrable, indestructible, and confident. This is the adamantine quality of the open mind. When you wear the armor of space, nothing can hurt you. Imagine a mind that is infinite and unrestricted, buoyant, and spontaneous. This is the lightness of the open mind. Who wouldn't want a mind like this?

PRIMORDIAL EXPANSION

You know that the primordial contraction (the "original sin") feels like "I," "me," "mine." But what does the primordial opening, the relaxation of this primal cramp, feel like? It feels like love. Not conditional and grasping love, which you can always identify because it's so sticky and self-referential, but unconditional and *selfless* love. If you prefer religious language, it feels like God. The intimidating topic of emptiness (and its colloquial rendering as openness) that we discussed earlier can now be seen in a warmer light. Emptiness is just a funny way to talk about love. Love and its expression as kindness, compassion, and selflessness is the affective expression of openness. Love is applied emptiness.

The vast power of unconditional love is one reason we're all afraid to open to such a degree, and for the ego to release its grip on itself. Being fully open means being vulnerable. It means "you" (the ego) can get hurt. To be so open, transparent, and utterly available is too much for the contracted ego to bear.

Ego and love, or contraction and openness, are mutually exclusive. Which means ego and emptiness are mutually exclusive. Ego is anti-emptiness. You can't fall deeply into real love and maintain your contracted ego. Ego is terrified of being that open, so it maintains the primordial contraction as a form of ultimate self-defense. But armed with the right view, you'll discover that when you're so open, you do feel things more, but they hurt you less. When you're not so solid and contracted, feelings don't have a place to land. Without any ground to take root, prapañca transforms into *nisprapañca*, or "freedom from conceptual elaboration." You feel things more fully and purely than ever, but because you're not feeding (contracting) them back to a feeler, they don't hurt. You don't take things personally, because you don't take them at all.

This returns us to the importance of right view. If you know in your heart that when you open and fall into reality that you're falling into love, it inspires you to release your grip. The purpose of the meditations in this book is to enable you to replace ego with eco, a self-centered approach with an other-centered approach, which is equivalent to a centerless and selfless approach—an approach based on love.

✤INSTRUCTION

The implications of developing open awareness will start to fall into place once you actually engage the practice. And when you get the hang of open awareness, you'll be able to practice this meditation anywhere and anytime, without a preparatory practice. But initially, it helps to slow things down with a few minutes of sitting meditation. If your mind is racing, it can stampede over the subtlety of a state of open awareness. We tend to lose the mind's essential openness in its rapid display, so it helps to lessen the display in order to recapture the essence.

The only modification with the shamatha instruction is to close your eyes, which helps to gather the mind and heighten the contrast. If you wear glasses, take them off. It's also good to be in a spacious room, or somewhere that allows you to look onto an open vista. Take your seat and ground yourself in your body and breath. As before, when something distracts you, notice the distraction, label it "thinking," and return to body and breath.

Open awareness nurtures an exquisite sensitivity to your body and mind, and a level of perception that allows you to detect very subtle contractions. I grew up on the shores of Lake Michigan, where storms created waves reaching nearly thirty feet. It would have taken a comet plunging into these rough waters to make any sort of splash. But just inland from the lake was a small pond. The water was so still that you could see the ripples from a tiny insect alighting on its surface. By settling the mind through referential meditation, you're shifting from the surface chop of Lake Michigan to the placidity of the pond, where even the tiniest pebble would make a discernible splash.

INSTRUCTION (CONTINUED)

Once you feel somewhat settled (you don't have to attain complete pacification to gain insights from open awareness), gently open your eyes and keep your gaze down. Leave your visual field unfocused. Now slowly raise your gaze until you are looking directly ahead. Notice how your eyes tend to stick to things during this transition. The mind's eye and the physical eye have a revelatory relationship, and you're going to use the latter to work with the former. Are your eyes sticky because your mind is sticky? You might notice a change in this visual tackiness as you develop proficiency in the practice.

When you're finally looking straight ahead, relax and open your visual field by "focusing" on the periphery. This decentralizes your gaze, inviting a quality of receptivity and accommodation. You're using the body (the eyes) to work with the mind. Notice how this open visual field invokes an openness of mind. If you find yourself closing down and focusing on an object in front of you, that's okay. Observe that, and then relax the focus. If something moves in your visual field and grabs your attention, just notice that and let it go. Relax . . . open. Relax . . . open. That's the "mantra" of this meditation.

Next, let your jaw relax and drop open. From the outside you might look like a stupefied idiot, staring wide-eyed and open-mouthed, but this posture is hardly idiotic. It's the asana (posture) of openness.

One of my teachers, Khenpo Tsültrim Gyamtso Rinpoche, would teach for hours on end without any notes, day after day, week after week. I studied with him for fourteen years, at annual retreats that sometimes lasted a month. As the interpreter would translate, Rinpoche would often look straight ahead, relax his jaw, and assume this stupefied posture. I often wondered, "What on earth is he doing!?" He clearly wasn't spacing out, because as soon as the translator stopped, Rinpoche would lower his gaze, close his mouth, and start teaching again, picking up right where he left off. It's just my guess, but I finally reflected that he might have been opening and settling his mind into that mirror-like surface, where drops of insight would land, and the ripples would be expressed as his teaching.

INSTRUCTION (CONTINUED)

The next step is to drop the reference points of body and breath. If something distracts you, you no longer return to your body or breath, as with referential meditation. Cut the anchor and allow your mind to drift to whatever arises. If you're drawn to a sound, for example, allow your mind to alight on that. The practice is to let your mind go there but without running commentary on the sound or capitulating to the usual proliferation (prapañca) that occurs when the mind is drawn to something. Let's say you hear the sound of a jet. Don't let the jet carry you away in a contrail of commentary: "Man, that plane is loud! I wonder where it's going? Safer to drive, in my opinion. 9/11 was such a tragedy. How did we ever get by without planes? Why are flights so damn expensive these days? I wonder how many gallons of fuel are being used . . ." If the mind drifts from the sound into a commentary about the sound, then it's okay to rest your mind on that. Briefly alight on the thoughts, which now become your new object of meditation. But don't get sucked into those thoughts.

As you progress into open awareness, pay refined attention to what you feel. What do you notice in your body as you start to open up? Are the transitions you undergo inviting or threatening? Is there part of you that doesn't want to feel open and exposed? Don't judge what you feel; just notice without commentary. You're practicing self-observation without judgment.

A smell might arise. Be open to that. Allow your mind to go to that. The smell briefly becomes the object of your meditation. But again, don't get swept up in the usual discursiveness that accompanies sensory input. If you do get swept away, rest on top of that. Let your mind go to the thoughts, but don't indulge them.

When you rest your awareness on a thought, it usually melts on contact, like a snowflake falling on a hot rock. If another snowflake arises, rest on that. You're not trying to melt the thought, but to let the thought naturally dissolve in the light of awareness. In technical terms, thought then "self-liberates."

Left alone, thoughts are never the problem. Sticking to the thought (and getting swept away by an avalanche of thinking) is the problem.

When we're drawn to something—a sound, sight, thought, or whatever—we usually grasp onto it. That stickiness is a form of contraction. The practice of open awareness is to "catch and release." Catch yourself contracting and proliferating, then let go. The meditation master Chökyi Nyima Rinpoche teaches that with this practice, attention should rest "free from focus, in a total openness free from reference point" and should remain "totally undisturbed by emotions, thoughts, and concepts." Thoughts and emotions only disturb us if we give them a place to land, take root, and grow. Remember, nothing can land on space.

In the practice of referential meditation, you may have been constantly distracted from your body and breath. Diversion is a central challenge in shamatha. In the practice of open awareness, however, *distraction becomes your meditation*. Nothing can interrupt this meditation because interruption becomes your meditation. Your mind can now accommodate anything. Open awareness puts a welcome mat in front of your mind and an exit sign on the back.

As with the nature of space itself, everything that arises in open awareness is allowed to come and go. The Zen master Hui Hai taught:

> Should your mind wander away, do not follow it, whereupon your wandering mind will stop wandering of its own accord. Should your mind desire to linger somewhere, do not follow it and do not dwell there, whereupon your mind's questing for a dwelling-place will cease of its own accord. Thereby, you will come to possess a non-dwelling mind—a mind which remains in the state of non-dwelling. If you are fully aware in yourself of a non-dwelling mind, you will discover that

there is just the fact of dwelling, with nothing to dwell upon or not to dwell upon. This full awareness in yourself of a mind dwelling upon nothing is known as having a clear perception of your own mind, or, in other words, as having a clear perception of your own nature.[4]

Hui Han's "non-dwelling mind" describes an aspect of open awareness that we could call "homeless awareness," meaning your mind is okay being anywhere, alighting briefly on whatever arises—finding temporary residence anyplace but never signing a lease. Everyplace and no-place become your home. The Buddha exemplified this non-dwelling (nonstick) mind. After attaining his enlightenment, he never again took up residence in the same place for more than a few months. He let his body and mind glide from one location to the next without attaching to anything.

INSTRUCTION (CONTINUED)

Until you become familiar with the practice of open awareness, stick to shorter sessions at first—maybe twenty minutes or so. One near enemy of open awareness, with its invitation to mix your mind with space, is spacing out. This is another practice that abides by the maxim "not too tight, not too loose," but it leans toward "too loose." As you try to loosen your contractions, it's easy to slip from spaciousness into spaciness. If you find yourself spacing out, briefly tighten your posture, and temporarily refocus your gaze. If you're really zoning out, you can either stand up for a few minutes to hit the refresh button, or just drop the whole thing and start again later. "Fresh start" is applicable to any meditation. Practice can get stale, and letting it all go is an antidote.

To close the meditation, centralize your vision by focusing straight ahead for a minute or so, close your mouth, then slowly lower your gaze. Notice how the transition back to referential meditation feels. Is it comforting to narrow your awareness, or does it feel confining? Does the familiarity of returning to form feel reassuring or claustrophobic? When your gaze is about six feet down in front of you, rest your vision there for a minute, then close your eyes and return your awareness to body and breath. How does it feel to "reincarnate" back into form? Do you notice how the openness "perfumes" your referential meditation? Do you feel lighter, freer, less encumbered?

Continue sitting in referential meditation for a few minutes; then open your eyes, but keep your gaze down. Then slowly look up, and move your head around. Does your world look or feel any different? Do a minute of standing meditation before transitioning back to life. If you move too quickly, or mindlessly, it's easy to leave your meditative mind on the cushion. You're trying to mix awareness with space, and to eventually mix your meditation with life. Just as the formal practice of open awareness accommodates whatever arises, you eventually want to bring your entire life "onto the cushion."

The Buddhist scholar Alan Wallace shares these tips:

> It is helpful for any kind of practice to know what the extremes are so you can cleave a middle path between them. For this one, if you try too hard this gives rise to agitation and if you don't try hard enough you fall into dullness. Once you recognize the two extremes, you want to do something in between, which means bouncing off of those extremes more and more lightly. If you are focusing on any object, a thought or an image, this is one extreme, on the agitation side. The other extreme, which is more elusive, is sitting there

with a blank mind not aware of anything. You are not attending to any object—just vegetating. What is in between is a quality of freshness because you are located in the present moment and vividly aware. You are not attending to any object at all but are aware that awareness is happening. It is wonderfully simple but subtle. It is like slipping into an old pair of shoes. When you are in it, you really know you are there. You need to develop a confidence that you know when you are doing it correctly. This is how it is done.[5]

INSTRUCTION (CONTINUED)

If you like to journal, it can be helpful to write down your experience and see how things change the more you do this meditation. Because open awareness is foreign to many people, it takes a while to get used to it. Everybody fumbles around at first, so be patient. Don't try too hard to do it perfectly. At a certain point the practice starts to "do you." Instead of automatically defaulting into contraction, you'll find yourself defaulting into openness.

CHAPTER 9

REFINEMENTS TO OPEN AWARENESS

The perfect person employs the mind like a mirror—it
receives, but it does not keep; it allows, but it does not grasp.

—CHUANG TZU

Our suffering is not redundant: it is part of what
happens when we try to figure out what is going on.

—BERNARDO KASTRUP

The "habituation to openness" that develops with open awareness
meditation represents a transition toward the natural state of the
mind and is a practice of radical acceptance (a virtue Buddhists call
the Great Equanimity) that will become increasingly natural to you.
You'll eventually find yourself having no preference toward anything
that comes up in meditation, and eventually in life. Everything you
encounter will have the quality of what the Mahāmudrā tradition
calls *one taste*, the same flavor of basic goodness. Using theistic
language, everything eventually "tastes like God" or (alternatively)
like Dzogchen's "perfect purity." It's pure because it's free of tasteless

conceptual proliferation. Whether you hear the lovely sound of a chirping bird or the jarring blast of a siren, you relate to them equally. Whether you smell a fragrant rose or rancid butter, it all starts to smell the "same." If you feel an ache in your knee or a warmth in your heart, it is all of one touch. This doesn't mean you can't discriminate between things. Your ability to differentiate is actually more refined than ever. It means you no longer discriminate *against* things.

GETTING UNSTUCK

Open awareness is another practice (like sitting meditation) that is both diagnostic and prescriptive, revealing just how sticky the mind is. You can begin to use this stickiness as a trigger to open. As you replace grasping with releasing, you'll be letting go of your grip on the ego itself, which allows you to fall into reality—and into love. Open awareness is therefore a prescription for transcending the ego, the mother of all contractions. Every time you replace contraction with relaxation, you're replacing the personal ego with transpersonal awareness.

When open awareness is brought to fruition, the gummy mind is replaced with a glossy mind. You'll start to release your attachment to ideologies and beliefs, and all sorts of tacky storylines. No need to "stick to your story" once you discover the story itself is a product of stickiness. The philosopher David Loy proposes that sometimes our tendency to grasp for meaning and truth is in fact "another attempt to ground ourselves by fixating on certain concepts that are believed to give us an effective fix on the world."[1] By contrast, he suggests, with open awareness we celebrate "the freedom of a mind that is not afraid of contradiction and so is able to dance in a coincidence of opposites, which is the way our minds naturally work when they do not stick."[2] By learning how to open our minds, we nurture "a nonabiding wisdom that can wander freely among truths since it does not need to fixate on any of them, for [. . .] nondwelling mind does not stick on any of the six sense-objects, and that includes mind-objects."[3]

We relate to others the way we relate to ourselves, so developing this equanimity opens our minds and hearts to the world. Open awareness is a mental yoga that stretches the mind to the point where it can wrap itself around everything without grasping after anything. It nurtures a flexibility that allows awareness to flow gracefully from one event to the next, like a flexible yogi moving fluidly from one pose to another. In their study of the lasting personality traits that can result from meditation, the neuroscientist Richard Davidson and the psychologist Daniel Goleman share a story about the Dalai Lama that demonstrates the remarkable emotional fluidity that the spiritual leader has attained through a lifetime of meditation. "Richie once saw tears begin to stream down the Dalai Lama's face as he heard about a tragic situation in Tibet," they relate as they set the scene:

> And then, a few moments later, the Dalai Lama noticed someone in the room doing something funny and he began laughing. There was no disrespect for the tragedy that brought him to tears, but rather, a buoyant and seamless transition from one emotional note to the next. . . . The Dalai Lama's emotional life seems to include a remarkably dynamic range of strong and colorful emotions, from intense sadness to powerful joy. His rapid, seamless transitions from one to another are particularly unique—this swift shifting betokens a lack of stickiness. . . . The stickiness spectrum runs from being utterly stuck, unable to free ourselves from distressing emotions or addictive wants, to the Dalai Lama's instant freedom from any given affect. One trait that emerges from living without getting stuck seems to be an ongoing positivity, even joy. When the Dalai Lama once was asked what had been the happiest point in his life, he answered, "I think right now."[4]

Three points from this excerpt warrant commentary. First, the equanimity that the Dalai Lama embodies, "from intense sadness to powerful joy," suggests that practices such as open awareness do not flatten the energies of life. Open awareness meditation is not about smacking every emotion into submissive equanimity. It nurtures appropriate emotional expression, not inappropriate repression.

To put that another way, open awareness cultivates awareness— emotional energies are actually heightened. Open awareness brings a sense of feeling more emotionally alive, more in touch with feelings, but less emotionally reactive. Emotions are purified of the reactive concepts generated by relentless self-reference. Emotions become cleaner, more honest and direct, because they're no longer sullied by the stains of conceptual proliferation, prapañca. This brings freedom to respond from an open mind and heart rather than a contracted stance. Defensive and offensive reactivity are replaced by graceful receptivity.

In regard to prapañca, all three of the core meditations we're exploring in this book—referential meditation, open awareness, and the reverse meditations—act as a filtration and purification system, sifting out the debris of conceptuality. All three practices clear the space so we can live more fully and cleanly. Our susceptibility to pollution is not just an external affair. The inner space of the mind can be poisoned too, with all manner of toxic commentary. Purification of that inner space begins with referential meditation, continues with open awareness, and reaches fruition in the reverse meditations.

The second point to note in this excerpt is "the Dalai Lama's *instant* freedom from any given affect." Open awareness allows us to release things on the spot. The ultimate freedom of an awakened one, a buddha, is born from just this practice. "Buddha" is sometimes translated as the "opened one" (in our present terms, that might correspond to the "unstuck one"), and that epithet refers to this ultimate freedom. That big freedom comes from all the small moments of opening.

By opening again and again, as the Dalai Lama seems to do, you're cultivating the Buddha mind. Or if that language doesn't speak to you, you're practicing the God mind, the basically good mind. The "opened ones" aren't attached to anything.

The third point is the extraordinary statement about the Dalai Lama's unconditional happiness; how many people would unhesitatingly answer that their happy place is right now? With practices like open awareness, you too can find the happiest point in your life in each and every moment, even when those moments feel really low. The relevance of open awareness gets more practical, and profound, the deeper you go.

Toward the end of his long life, the sage Jiddu Krishnamurti was asked, "What is the secret to your happiness?" His reply was disarmingly simple: "I don't mind what happens." The practice of open awareness *is* the practice of "I don't mind what happens." A sound arises? I don't mind. A smell occurs? I don't mind. Whatever happens, I simply don't mind.

A near enemy to the attainment of great equanimity, however, is the ease with which this attitude can slide into an attitude of "I don't *care* what happens." Disinterestedness liberates and can help us detach (differentiate) from the sticky contents of our mind. But at the same time, healthy differentiation always has the potential to degrade into pathological dissociation or into dismissiveness. In attempting to distance ourselves from the contents of our mind, we can slide into a sterile relationship to our thoughts and emotions. With open awareness, thoughts and emotions are seen as ornaments of the mind—something to celebrate and then release.

CONTEMPLATION

Think of three instances in your life when you were really happy. Bring them vividly to mind. Maybe it was your wedding day, the birth of your child, or when you bought your first home. Now see if you can find a common denominator behind each of these occasions. Is there an *unconditional* ingredient tucked into every instance of happiness? The common denominator behind any instance of happiness is your full presence to what's happening. On your wedding day, or at the birth of your child, you weren't spinning off into the past or future, diluting the experience. The power of the experience bolted you into the present moment. You were fully present and open to what was happening—qualities to which we append the label "happiness."

UNCONDITIONAL HAPPINESS

What we've just seen in the discussion of equanimity and disinterestedness is that the practice of open awareness doubles as a practice of unconditional happiness. This is not the usual version of happiness, which is conditional. We're normally happy when certain conditions are met, and then spend our lives trying to sustain or reestablish those conditions. We then become slaves to external circumstance. I'm happy when I'm drinking a margarita and watching a glorious sunset on the beaches of the Yucatan. But where does that happiness go when the beaches are littered with seaweed, the sky is cloudy, or the margarita tastes bad? Open awareness allows us to be happy on a cloudy day, at a soiled beach, with a bad drink. We can raise a toast to even that.

CONTEMPLATION

Bring to mind three instances when you were miserable. Maybe it was when you got divorced, lost your job, or had to foreclose on your house. Bring these painful memories vividly to mind. Now see if you can find a common denominator to each moment of unhappiness. If you do this, you will discover that in each instance, there was an inability to contain the experience, an unwillingness to say "yes" to what was happening. We suffer in direct proportion to our inability to accommodate experience. When things get difficult, we often say, "I don't have room for this," or "I don't have time for this," or "I can't deal with this." We contract against the unwanted experience, which makes it even more unwanted. With open awareness, radical acceptance becomes your protection. This doesn't mean you naïvely acquiesce and no longer act to improve your life. It means you also work to improve your relationship to life.

Look into any instance of happiness and you will find a quality of openness. Look into any instance of unhappiness and you will find a quality of contraction. By replacing contraction with expansion, open awareness replaces unhappiness with unconditional happiness. Perhaps *joy* is a better word. Charlotte Joko Beck writes in *Now Zen*, "Joy isn't something we have to find. Joy is who we are if we're not preoccupied with something else." Imagine what your life would be like if you could truly say, "I don't mind what happens."

The natural state of the mind is to be open, and therefore unconditionally happy. When you contract, a strain is created as you stretch away (dis-tract) from the natural state. It's a pull that is felt as the many levels of unhappiness, like stress, anxiety, pressure, worry, unease, apprehension, or any other feeling that longs to be resolved. In other words, the tension generated by contraction is felt as the longing for happiness. You long for some kind of release, which results in the many forms of substitute, or conditional, happiness. But because the release is a substitute— like drugs, alcohol, sex, consumerism, or virtually everything else we do in our misguided quest for resolution—it never truly satisfies. The teacher Rupert Spira, writing on the nondual nature of consciousness, summarizes that quest in this way:

> The contraction of awareness into a finite mind exerts a tension on itself which is always seeking to be relieved, just as the compression of a rubber ball sets up an inevitable tension that is always trying to expand or relax into its

original neutral condition. This contraction of awareness is felt as the experience of suffering, and the inexorable force toward the natural state of equilibrium is felt as the desire for freedom, peace, and happiness. Thus, the desire for happiness is simply the mind's desire to be divested of its limitations and return to its inherently relaxed [and open state]. . . . The search for enlightenment is simply a refinement of the desire for happiness. It is an indication that the search has become conscious rather than simply instinctive.[5]

The question is this: Is it better to scratch the itch or to return to a condition free of the rash? Open awareness returns you to the natural itchless state.

AWARENESS OF AWARENESS

The investigation of nondual insights that ends this chapter is a subtle but big step forward in the refinement of open awareness. If it doesn't land with you, don't worry. It's not for everybody. But for intrepid explorers, the instructions that follow add extra depth to open awareness practice that can change the way you perceive everything—including your pain. This deeper aspect goes to the heart of the Indic concepts of samsāra and nirvāṇa: when awareness sticks to something and then proliferates (prapañca), the result is samsāra; when awareness glides across the same things, it leads to nirvāṇa. Perfect purity also takes on new meaning in this context, because pure awareness is that which doesn't dwell on anything. It's not stained by anything because it doesn't stick to anything long enough to get soiled. Conversely, impure attention is sticky attention that soils itself by grounding onto things.

The following instructions will be asking you to transition from duality into nonduality in a way that demands close attention toward the nature of perception. What makes this transition slippery is that the sharp looking it requires is conjoined with soft openness. Openness and relaxation are key, and by themselves can lead to nondual discoveries. But the interjection of subtle investigations can grease the skids. The following refinements will take you to the limits of conceptuality and to the edge of duality. It's like walking to the rim of a diving board and taking the leap. Your investigation will also leave a metaphoric trail of breadcrumbs, allowing you to find your way back home to your nondual nature.

Open awareness at this refined level pulsates between a subtle concentration of awareness (as you bring incisive analysis into the perceptual process) alternating with a relaxation and openness (as you release your focus). In so doing you'll be alternating between relative (concentrative) and absolute (expansive) techniques.

❋INSTRUCTION

Start your meditation as before, with several minutes of sitting in referential shamatha to settle your mind. Nondual insights are very "quiet," and you'll need the silence of referential meditation, and the space of open awareness, to detect these nuances. We're setting up two high-resolution contrast mediums: the stasis of referential shamatha, which facilitates the perception of the movement of mind; and the openness of open awareness, which further facilitates the perception of extremely subtle contractions. We're going to take previously unconscious processes and bring them into the light of consciousness.

Referential shamatha and open awareness are akin to creating the super-polished mirrors on a high-powered telescope like the Hubble or Webb, a surface so smooth that it allows light to be purely reflected without any deviations.[6] In this case, it is the light of awareness itself that you want to reflect off the "objects" of your perceptions, without any deviations, so that you can see things purely.

INSTRUCTION (CONTINUED)

When you feel settled (or somewhat "polished"), slowly raise your gaze, open your visual field, and drop the referents of body and breath, as before. Mix your mind with space-awareness.

The following instructions, which are a form of analytic meditation (vipashyana), interrupt the practice at first. It's like guiding the telescope to focus on a specific star. Shifting metaphors, the refinements are like a skilled attorney who leads a witness in the direction they want them to go. They lead you away from duality and toward nondual insights.

INSTRUCTION (CONTINUED)

Up to this point in the practice, you've allowed your mind to freely roam from one sensory experience to another, whether it's sight, sound, smell, taste, touch, or thought. (In Buddhist psychology, the mind consciousness is considered a sense consciousness, on equal footing with your five physical sense consciousnesses.) Now, as awareness glides across these six consciousnesses, pay very close attention to what's happening when you're sensing something. Do you assume that "I'm hearing that sound," or "I'm seeing that object," or "I'm having that thought"? Does it seem like you're aware of an external object (even if that object is a thought); that you're in here perceiving an object out there? Perceiving things in terms of subject and object is just the way it is. But is it? Is appearance in harmony with reality? Am I truly perceiving that? Let's feel into this more.

In an unexamined way, it does appear that your mind is making contact with an external object. But if you pay very close attention with your polished mirror, you will discover that as awareness perches upon a sensory object, it's actually alighting onto nothing. It's landing on no-thing. Nothing but awareness itself. Pay attention, and you will detect a very subtle series of contractions that generate the illusion that there is an object out there, and by immediate implication, a subject in here. It's the contraction itself that generates the illusion that there is a thing—and an "out there."

The elusive and lightning-fast primary contraction, which freezes awareness into an object, has been going on for so long that it seems to be a given. The secondary and tertiary contractions then generate the equally fast commentary (prapañca) that accompanies the primary contraction (that there's a thing out there), which serves to further solidify the primary contraction (by referring it to other concepts and contractions). This commentary acts as subconscious gossip, and like all gossip, it serves to validate our impressions. We gossip as a way to substantiate our view of things. In this case, the uncertain impression that there even is a thing.

Why are we bothering with all this? Because this same process occurs every single time we contract onto unwanted sensory stimulation, freezing it into this thing we call "pain." Then the instantaneous secondary and tertiary contractions generate this thing we call "suffering." This refinement of open awareness takes us back to the source of all our suffering and allows us to deconstruct it.

To detect all this, you allow the secondary and tertiary contractions to open and release. You drop the storylines (in Sanskrit, these are termed *savikalpa*—"with thought construct") and return to the raw sensory perception (*nirvikalpa*—"without thought construct"), over and over. The commentary is overtly or covertly self-referential: "How does this sound relate to me?" or "What is this feeling I'm perceiving?" or any of the infinite spins you put on what you perceive. The self-referential commentary also works to further solidify the formless initial perception (nirvikalpa) into some form, a thing out there. Remember that to deconstruct is to deautomatize. To deconstruct duality, you have to deautomatize these instantaneous contractions and return to what triggers them, to what's really happening.

What's actually happening is that the lightning-fast primary contraction is mistaken for an object. Awareness itself is freezing onto sensory input. This is the birth of the sense of "other," that there's something "out there." In the same instant that the sound is perceived "out there," you are generated "in here" (we're back to the creation of the sense of self, the result of the primordial contraction), and you then come to the mistaken conclusion that "I am hearing that." No, you're not. It just appears that way. As the nondual Hindu traditions proclaim, tat tvam asi: "Thou art that." The sound is hearing itself. The Zen master Dogen famously wrote, "I came to realize clearly that mind is no other than mountains and rivers and the great wide earth, the sun and the moon and the stars."

INSTRUCTION (CONTINUED)

Slow down, take a deep breath, and then take a very close look. You have to do this again and again, so be patient. You're trying to reverse your automatic "contractual" relationship to appearance. That's not easy. So relax, take your time, and be exquisitely open to what you perceive.

Bernardo Kastrup writes, "Most people can't or won't go there; the mere attempt exposes them to what I like to call the 'vertigo of eternity': the appalling realization that what is actually going on is not even commensurable with what they think is going on."[7]

You have to keep the aperture of your awareness open long enough, through repeated sessions, to see what's actually going on. It's like stepping outside of a brightly lit room and into the dark night. At first you can't see a thing. Your pupils (awareness) are so contracted you can't see. But if you're patient and keep your eyes open long enough, your pupils dilate and you start to see things never seen before. You start to discern unconscious processes that have always been there, hiding in the darkness of ignorance. The practice of open awareness dilates your consciousness, opening the aperture of your mind.[8]

INSTRUCTION (CONTINUED)

To finish the instruction: when you alight onto a sensory consciousness, try to stay ever so lightly with consciousness itself, the initial formless awareness (the real news), before it contracts into the false sense of being the awareness of an object (the fake news). Avoid the temptation to get sucked into the secondary and tertiary conceptual contractions, the prapañca. (Or better yet, just briefly rest awareness on that, the mental sixth consciousness, and the prapañca melts on contact.)

Khenpo Rinpoche explains, "When a visual form is first perceived, there is no experience of anything other than the visual consciousness itself. In other words, one does not experience the existence or nonexistence of an object. What is experienced is completely within the realm of visual consciousness, but the clarity or radiance of the experience is mistaken to be an external object."[9]

If the primary contraction is awareness freezing onto sensory input, the secondary and tertiary contractions are icing on this frozen cake. The practice is therefore de-icing, and returning to raw sensory perception. Your proficiency in the practice of referential meditation comes into play here, but instead of coming back again and again to body and breath, you open, release, and come back to whatever is arising—to formless awareness itself. Thrangu Rinpoche lends a hand,

> As far as the way things appear to function, there is definitely the appearance in our experience of external objects that are encountered by the sense organs, producing consciousness or awareness of those objects. Actually, what we perceive as external objects and what we perceive as the internal faculties are really aspects of the consciousnesses themselves. For example, when your eyes see form, what we would normally say occurs is that there is an external object that your eyes are capable of encountering; through the encounter between the eye and the object, a visual consciousness is generated. From the point of view of the way things are, what you perceive as external form is the objective or lucid aspect of the visual consciousness itself; i.e., eye consciousness appears as form. The emptiness aspect of the eye consciousness is what you experience as, or presume to be, the subject experiencing an object.[10]

INSTRUCTION (CONTINUED)

If you find yourself automatically thinking about thinking, instead of thinking about the object, then you just alight onto that thinking. This practice may seem complicated, but it's actually very simple. It's just hard to put into words. Think about how hard it is for a child who is first learning to walk. And imagine how complicated it would be to explain to that child "how to do it." Instead, what happens is that they fall over again and again, but finally they get the hang of it, and walking becomes second nature. Open awareness is actually the natural state of an open mind. It doesn't take long before you start to catch on. It only feels unnatural because you've been so contracted for so long. Simply open your mind, and rest briefly on whatever arises. All these discoveries naturally unfold as the mind unwinds, and the contractions self-liberate.

Because the investigation is so subtle, it works best in short sessions, repeated often. If you try to stay with the analysis too long, the mind can get stale. To keep it crisp, look sharply, like striking a gong. Then open, relax, and rest in the tone that follows that strike. If you try too hard, contraction sneaks back in. It's a high-wire act, where finding your balance between not too tight and not too loose is key.

Writing about nonduality is difficult, because language is inherently dualistic. How can the finite relate to infinity, or the temporal to eternity? It can't. When the dualistic mind tries to wrap itself around nonduality, the result is often irony, paradox, or bewilderment. This is when we have to blow our minds open if we want to find a path to end our suffering—or in Buddhist terms, to reach nirvāṇa. *Nirvāṇa* means "to extinguish, blow out," and the above instructions are designed to blow the conceptual mind into nonconceptual smithereens.

If nonduality is so subtle, why bother? Because everything in our gross lives arises from these subtle processes. We're working with the "genetic" basis of samsāra here, and we can cure a host of fully manifested dis-eases by working our way down to their origins. (Thoreau had a similar intention, when he went into retreat to "shave close, to drive life into a corner, and reduce it to its lowest terms.") This work will meet its ultimate refinement in the reverse meditations, where the threefold evolution of open awareness comes to fruition. You have progressed from appearances arising *to* awareness, then appearances arising *in* awareness, and finally appearances arising *as* awareness. With this transition from dualistic perception to nondualistic perception, you'll now use reverse meditation to alter your relationship to pain. In so doing, you'll discover nirvāṇa in samsāra, and heaven in a new understanding of hell.

CHAPTER 10

THE REVERSE MEDITATIONS

Some Preliminaries

Well, then, love your suffering. Do not resist it, do not flee from it. It is your aversion that hurts, nothing else.

—HERMANN HESSE

There is no birth of consciousness without pain.

—CARL JUNG

We're finally ready to dive into the reverse meditations proper. These practices deliver a number of surprises, beginning with the fact that with these meditations you're not stretching *up* toward the heavens, or *out* toward conventional feel-good spirituality. With the reverse meditations you're reaching *down* toward the earth, and *in* toward unconventional real-good spirituality. Chögyam Trungpa said, "There is no way out. The magic is to discover that there is a way in." The reverse meditations provide the way in. This chapter is rich in supporting statements to buttress the radical claims, for as the maxim goes: extraordinary claims require extraordinary evidence.

Consisting of four steps, these iconoclastic, gritty meditations have stretched me open, allowing me to embrace any experience. They have also helped me understand the phenomenon of contraction at entirely new levels. But they're not for everybody. On one level, like any meditation, they are optional. But is pain optional? Are unwanted experiences optional? Are old age, sickness, and death optional? For those who want a healthier relationship to these inevitable lifetime partners, and long for ways to bring pain onto the path, the reverse meditations are a treasure.

Although I learned these practices within the context of the Mahāmudrā tradition, they can also be held within the framework of the charnel ground meditations described in chapter 4. Charnel grounds, you may recall, are those wretched and revolting places that elicit intense reactivity and contraction. They're hell on earth. But as the Buddhist scholar Hamid Sardar has said, "In tantra, hell is paradise."[1] The reverse meditations are tantric in spirit.

The reverse meditations also have doctrinal footing in other Buddhist schools. In the Mahāyāna tradition, for instance, reverse meditations have a precursor in the practice of *tonglen*, or "sending and taking."[2] In tonglen practice, you reverse the egoic logic of always putting yourself first. Using the medium of the breath, you breathe in all the pain and suffering of the world, and you breathe out love and peace. You take in darkness and send out light.[3] Tonglen itself is part of the Tibetan Buddhist *lojong* teachings, or the "seven points of mind training." Lojong practice consists of fifty-nine slogans—such as "Drive all blames into one," which teaches us to take responsibility for our actions, and "Gain and victory to others, loss and blame to oneself"—notable for their strategies of reversal. From a Hīnayāna perspective, the *Nine Cemetery Contemplations* (from the *Satipaṭṭhāna Sutta*) offer another prelude, as one contemplates the graphic disintegration of the body after death, reversing our usual avoidance strategies around the end of life.

The practice of open awareness showed you how to open to anything that arises—cultivating the "I don't mind what happens" attitude—and the reverse meditations follow elegantly from that practice. Reginald Ray writes that in the open awareness of meditation, "No matter how tormented our state of mind just prior to touching in to this state, once we are there all of our pain and suffering is experienced in a new light."[4] The reverse meditations tag-team with open awareness to create an indestructible crucible for transformation, allowing you to place all your unwanted experiences in a liberating new light. In cultivating this industrial strength meditation, you're also inviting a deeper understanding of contraction, for never is contraction more evident than when you're in pain.

You've seen that authentic spirituality isn't about feeling good (unless you're talking about basic goodness). It's about getting real. The psychologist Robert Augustus Masters shares his views about the earthiness of authentic spirituality:

> True spirituality is not a high, not a rush, not an altered state. It has been fine to romance it for a while, but our times call for something far more real, grounded, and responsible; something radically alive and naturally integral; something that shakes us to our very core until we stop treating spiritual deepening as something to dabble in here and there. Authentic spirituality is not some little flicker or buzz of knowingness, not a psychedelic blast-through or a mellow hanging-out on some exalted plane of consciousness, not a bubble of immunity, but a vast fire of liberation, an exquisitely fitting crucible and sanctuary, providing both heat and light for the healing and awakening we need.[5]

Masters then exhorts us to realize that real practice "asks that we cease turning away from our pain, numbing ourselves, and expecting spirituality to make us feel better."[6]

The classic comfort plan of New Age spirituality, which touts the importance of unity and Oneness, often does so by reinforcing "fragmentation by separating out from and rejecting what is painful, distressed, and unhealed; all the far-from-flattering aspects of being human," says Masters.[7] Spiritual shoppers are okay with Oneness, as long as it means becoming one with what feels good, or following your bliss.[8] But to really grow, you have to turn toward "the painful, disfigured, ostracized, unwanted, or otherwise disowned aspects of ourselves and cultivate as much intimacy as possible with them," as Masters says.[9] Who in their right mind wants to do *that*?

The cognitive scientist Scott Barry Kaufman writes, "Healthy transcendence doesn't stem from an attempt at distracting oneself from displeasure with reality. Healthy transcendence involves *confronting* reality as it truly is, head on, with equanimity and loving kindness."[10] An authentic path, he says, is "not about leaving any parts of ourselves or anyone else behind or singularly rising above the rest of humanity"[11]—or, I would add, our pain. In a similar vein, Masters points out a major limitation with the tranquility cultivated by mindfulness meditations, a pacification that readily turns into "metaphysical valium":

> Despite their undeniable calming and relaxing effects, meditative practices that sedate the mind can serve a detrimental purpose; *feeling greater calm and relaxation is not necessarily always a good thing*, particularly when it doesn't coexist with discernment and insight. Tranquilizers, meditative or otherwise, simply numb us, and if we have any investment in being numb, we may be drawn to meditative practices that keep us distant from our pain. As long as we are consciously and skillfully turning *toward* our pain and difficulties, staying close enough to them to work with them effectively, we will be less easily seduced by the desire to sedate ourselves.[12]

WHY THE REVERSE?

Reversing our normal strategies takes courage, but that's where transformation takes place. The psychologist Bruce Tift writes,

In my experience, the practices that carry the greatest potential for transformative change are usually counterinstinctual, meaning we don't want to do them, or they go against our basic evolutionary survival responses. To work with our neurotic defense mechanisms, we need the willingness to go into exactly those vulnerabilities— the fear, rage, grief, and horrible feelings—that we've spent decades dedicated to not feeling. But who wants to do that? Who wants to go into feeling stupid or abandoned? To sit with these feelings goes against our instincts.[13]

However, Tift urges that "it might be in our best interest (and perhaps in the interest of others) to do something so apparently stupid as to intentionally have a relationship with our pain and fear."[14]

With the gift of open awareness, you have opened to experience. With reverse meditation, you'll be taking the next step: reversing your defensive strategies and going directly into painful experience. Normally when you hurt, you want out. Your default is to anesthetize, to dis-tract from the ferocity of the experience, but paradoxically that distraction transforms pain into suffering. The analgesic industry (along with every form of substance abuse) and the entertainment industry (which is a form of analgesia) are billion-dollar success stories because they institutionalize and satisfy our longing for distraction from pain or boredom.

At the individual level, we dis-tract ourselves from the discomfort of boredom when we buy into discursive thinking. We get lost in the inner movies of the mind ("thought" in tantric language is actually referred to as "movement of mind"), which transport us away from boredom as effectively as any Hollywood production.

Referential shamatha and open awareness work to remove the diversions that dilute experience. The reverse meditations concentrate our experience even more, by inviting us directly into that discord that the diversions are designed to allay.

THE SPIRIT OF MATTER

The wisdom of right view is crucial at this point. Seeing through our pain and suffering, even at a philosophical level, is essential for going fully into pain and suffering. The reverse meditations hold the view of tantra, and one aspect of tantra is noteworthy for understanding these meditations: that is, the way tantra reclaims the value of matter—not for the sake of matter itself, but for the sake of using matter in a spiritual way. Tantra teaches that pain can be brought to the spiritual path, and heaven can in fact be found on earth.[15]

Trungpa Rinpoche taught about *negative negativity*: "The philosophies and rationales we use to justify avoiding our own pain. We would like to pretend that these 'evil' and 'foul-smelling' aspects of ourselves and our world are not really there, or that they should not be there."[16] Robert Masters expresses a similar idea: "Being negative about our negativity fragments us, stranding us from our unresolved wounds. Hurt, rage, grief, shame, fear, terror, loneliness, despair, and so on—all of these tend to get lumped together as 'negativity,' as something far from spiritual."[17] We try to escape from this negativity, but as Masters writes:

> All we've really done is escape from the very pain that, if fully felt and skillfully approached, would free us to live more deeply and more fully and yes, more spiritually. Our lack of intimacy with our anger, fear, shame, doubt, terror, loneliness, grief, and other painful states keeps our experience superficial, emotionally anemic, and addicted to whatever helps numb us to our negativity. . . .
>
> So turn toward your negativity. Stop pathologizing it, stop relegating it to a lower status, stop keeping it in the dark. Go to it, open its doors and windows, take it by the hand. Meet its gaze. Feel its woundedness, feel into it, feel for it, feel it without any buffers. Soon you will start to sense that its gaze is none other than your own, perhaps from an earlier time, but yours nonetheless, containing so much of you.[18]

We are attempting to cultivate "positive negativity," to see the gift in hardship and pain. The Sanskrit scholar Christopher Wallis points out that when someone is trying to avoid negative emotions and feelings, that person

> will not learn what that emotion has to teach if his only goal is to get back to feeling good as soon as possible. For such a person, the emotion will visit again and again, since he has failed to open to it as a teacher and, thus, has failed to integrate its energy. There is an enormous amount of energy locked in "negative" emotions that we cannot avail ourselves of without this basic self-acceptance. When we rise above self-condemnation and accept ourselves and what we are feeling, that energy naturally reveals its beneficial quality by pointing us to a deeper experience of our authentic nature. So let us drop this term "negative emotions" altogether, since it usually means "emotions we should not be having."[19]

Wallis exhorts us to get rid of the notion "that one state of mind is 'better' than another, and that you 'should' be feeling this way or that." Those who engage in tantric methods (*tantrikas*), "*must not fear pain or intense feeling of any kind or think it ungodly, or they cut themselves off from a huge source of life-energy.*" Tantrikas are sometimes called *viras*, "heroes" or "adepts," because it takes heroic courage to look clearly at our pain and not push it away, saying, "that's not me," but rather embrace its power.[20]

THE BODY AS A CRUCIBLE

In reverse meditation, the crucible for transformation is our body. Our body, our personal earth, is the ground of our experience that we need to return to. Sri Aurobindo said that the process of the path is the descent of the spirit into the flesh—embodiment more than transcendence. By "waking down" like this, and staying down, we stay in contact with the truth. Deception (let alone confabulation and catastrophizing) cannot follow you into your body.[21] The Hevajra Tantra in Tibetan Buddhism proclaims that "wisdom abides in the body." In Tibetan yoga, awakening is the result of greater and greater embodiment. Note how these stances are the reverse of most transcendental spiritual strategies. The philosopher Christopher Bache writes:

> The purpose of spiritual awakening appears to be not escaping from physical existence, as [the] earlier religions proposed, but awakening ever more completely *inside* physical existence . . . we are no longer running to explore a universe "out there," but rather are "calling down heaven," pulling higher states of awareness into our physical being, alchemically mixing heaven and earth in the vessel of our human body. When nirvāṇa (enlightenment) and samsāra (cyclic existence) are truly one . . . then heaven is realized on earth and there is no felt need to go elsewhere.[22]

When we're in physical or emotional pain, however, our default is to anesthetize ourselves by retreating into the conceptual mind. The entertainment business begins right here. To "enter-tain" is to "hold-between." Instead of staying with the difficult feeling, we contract away into easier thinking. We use thoughts to buffer us from the raw immediacy of our pain, holding our storylines between us and what hurts. Reginald Ray writes, "The more we shut out our body, the more we retreat into thinking. The intensity of our compulsive thinking is in direct proportion to the extent that we are unwilling to experience our body in a full and direct way. We have, in fact, dissociated from it."[23] If the body is the source of our pain, our default instinct is to get out of it.[24]

Many of us are so disconnected from our bodies, so physically numb, that we're not even aware of our numbness. We're so frozen that when we start to reconnect to reality, to our body, it can hurt. When your body-mind starts to defrost, things can get worse before they get better. Bache writes that pain "is part of a purification process, and therefore pain becomes our ally in the work. One learns to reverse one's instinct to avoid suffering and to open to it instead, not because we like to suffer but because of what lies on the other side of suffering."[25]

As you start to approach the truth of fully embodied experience, you'll find you're "getting warm." That warmth can eventually feel like a boiler as you begin the necessary de-icing. But it only feels painful because of the contrast.[26] If you weren't so frozen, the defrosting wouldn't hurt. "Within the framework of the body work," Ray says, "the *appearance of discomfort is thus good news*. This is because it marks the beginning of *reversing* the process . . . of the development and fortification of the ego, the ultimate cause of our disembodiment and alienation from the deeper self."[27] The conceptual ego is the icebox that freezes everything in its perverse attempts to keep us from feeling anything. The ego puts everything on ice—as a way to preserve itself.

The first brave step with the reverse meditations is moving from a state of "insentient numbness backward into a state of discomfort," Ray continues. "The discomfort becomes more subtle and transparent as we move deeper and deeper into the body, through each successive level of emotion, feeling, sensation, mood, and felt-sense. Finally, we arrive at our core, the empty space at the center, which is open and free but, at the same time, the basis of our entire being. At that point, our embodiment is complete, our realization is actual, and the solid 'ego' has become a distant dream."[28]

The de-icing is now complete.

INTEGRAL PAIN

The reverse meditations require an integral approach to pain—an approach that honors and incorporates the critical role of pain in sustaining physical evolution while also acknowledging the possibilities that pain offers for promoting psycho-spiritual growth. In the biological realm, pain is hardwired into our DNA as a signal that something is wrong. The "fight, flight, or freeze" response kicks in, and we do what we must to remove or avoid the pain. It's only because of this healthy response that we have evolved to the point where we can now contemplate the nature of pain, including its ability to focus the mind: because the experience itself is so concentrated, it concentrates attention. It's because pain is so concentrated, however, that we spend much of our lives trying to dilute it.

The problem occurs when we take this biological relationship and transpose it into the psycho-spiritual domain. Then the very pain that sustains physical evolution comes to retard psycho-spiritual growth. In the psychological and spiritual world, pain can be a signal that you're doing something *right*. You're "getting warm." As clichéd as it may be, there is validity to the saying "no pain, no gain." Without an integral understanding of pain, evolution flips into devolution. And any thought of engaging in the reverse meditations comes to a screeching halt.

So please be kind to yourself with these meditations. On one level, you're reversing the tide of physical evolution. Understanding this helps with the resistance that often arises to these practices. Moreover, ego steps in to further subvert the process. In other words, pain protects biological form. Ego is exclusive identification with form. When you're trying to evolve from ego to egolessness, from form to formlessness, this healthy spiritual impulse can feel like a biological threat. When you don't have a proper understanding of the ego, and its historical relationship to pain, ego barges in to protect itself and dissuade you from doing these reverse meditations.

In the spirit of alchemy and tantra, however, with the right view we can transform a central obstacle to (physical) evolution into a key opportunity for (spiritual) evolution—like transforming lead into gold, and poison into medicine. Ray continues, "Far from being a problem, [the discomfort] is what we have been looking for. If we believe that our discomfort is an indicator that something is wrong, it will be natural for us to resist it and push it back again into the shadows of the body. If, on the other hand, we see it for what it is—a positive development and marker of our progress . . . we are far more likely to welcome it and approach it with an attitude of openness and curiosity."[29] Discomfort, fear, pain, and a host of other unwanted experiences now point out precisely where we *need* to go if we want to grow.

I have used this radical advice—to follow my fear, my vulnerability, my pain—to guide much of my spiritual life. It's the reason I entered my challenging three-year retreat. I couldn't think of anything more frightful than facing my mind so directly for so long. It's the reason I do dark retreats. I can't think of anything more concentrated than being with myself so intensely.[30] And it's the reason I do these reverse meditations. This unconventional (reverse) approach, of following my fear, vulnerability, and pain, has been my most trustworthy guide for growth. But a caution about this growth: avoid becoming a spiritual thrill-seeker. Entering challenging situations in search of a spiritual rush is not meditation. The reverse meditations require the right view, guidance, and support that you have been building throughout this book.

As powerful as these practices are, they are not a panacea for the hardships of life. In the spirit of integral approaches, they should be used in concert with traditional methods for working with pain. Trauma therapy has a place, as do cognitive behavioral therapy, pharmaceuticals, and dozens of other pain management strategies. But the reverse meditations can augment, and at times completely replace, a host of conventional methods for working with pain at physical, psychological, and even spiritual levels.

THE SUFFERING EQUATION

For every unwanted experience, there's a reverse meditation. Undesirable circumstances are infinite, but the reverse meditations amount to a one-size-fits-all practice. You'll learn how to do this in a formal way in chapter 11, and I recommend practicing in formal sessions until you get the hang of it. But the power of these practices comes from their immediate applicability.

Because pain is arguably the most common unwanted experience, let's use it as our example. The journey into, and then *through*, your pain begins with a simple equation: suffering equals pain times resistance. By dropping your resistance to pain, you can remove your suffering. There's still this thing called pain, but your relationship to it is transformed. (As you'll see below, even "pain" is eventually deconstructed.)

A psychological angle helps extend the principles of reverse meditations into emotional pain: Carl Jung wrote, "Neurosis is a ready substitute for legitimate suffering." If you replace "intense experience" or "unwanted experience" for "legitimate suffering," you can see the universality of the reverse meditations, and the method to their madness.[31] By increasing your tolerance for experiential intensity, you decrease your need for neurosis. A further interpretation tags Jung's statement directly to the reverse meditations: "Suffering is a ready substitute for legitimate pain." So, let's get rid of your suffering by legitimizing your pain, which is accomplished by reversing your relationship to it.

Following the maxim "transcend but include," the reverse meditations build upon the earlier meditations of referential shamatha, open awareness, and a more sophisticated understanding of the wisdom of your body. The reverse meditations also take your "anti-complaint" meditation to a new level. These practices all support each other to create the fireproof crucible where you can transform the hellholes of life.

The reverse meditations are also gently held within the practice of loving-kindness (metta in Pali, maitri in Sanskrit), which may surprise some people. How is plunging into your pain being kind to yourself? The kindest thing you could ever do for yourself, and for others, is to speak and live the truth. Pain may not feel good, but it is real. And it is better to live a genuine life in stinging reality than a fantasy existence free of pain.

If you strive for a consistently "cool" life, you're living on a pilot-light level, and life will pass you by. Real spirituality means living with the gas fully on. Suzuki Roshi said, "When you do something, you should do it with your whole body and mind; you should be concentrated on what you do. You should do it completely, like a good bonfire. You should not be a smoky fire. You should burn yourself completely. If you do not burn yourself completely, a trace of yourself will be left in what you do."[32] Most of us like to "smoke," and smoking is hazardous to an authentic life. Instead of staying in the bonfires of life, we smolder over events, fume over affronts, and fret over endless personal insults.[33] We do so because we're not equipped with a crucible that can handle the heat.

The reverse meditations offer a method of cremating your experience as you live it—a method of lighting up your life. The Kashmir Shaivist master Kṣemarāja writes that when "something that is actually being experienced now, becomes one with the Fire of Consciousness through the process of 'sudden digestion,' also known as the method of 'total devouring,' then it is said to be *graced*, because it has been integrated into the state of complete fullness."[34] The exhortation from all the great masters is to consume and digest all of life, however bitter or sweet. Every other form of consumption is secondary and inauthentic—it never satisfies. Authentic consumerism is devouring life itself, and the reverse meditations ignite the Fire of Consciousness that can deep-fry and swallow it all.

THE NEUROSCIENCE OF MEDITATION AND PAIN

Ten years ago I spent most of a weekend in an fMRI (a neuroimaging device that measures brain changes in real time) at a renowned neuroscience lab that was studying pain in long-term meditators.[35] Lab technicians placed a wristband on my left arm that generated heat, ranging from room temperature to unbearably hot, then scanned my brain to see how I reacted to the onset of pain. The scientists differentiated three aspects of pain: the sensory aspect, the affective (emotional) aspect, and the cognitive aspect, or all the interpretations we bring to the raw sensation.[36] Like other studies, the one I participated in showed that meditation influences all three aspects, which lends credibility to the claims in this book.[37]

Evan Thompson summarized some of the results of these studies, concluding, "A general finding across all the long-term meditation practitioners, compared to the control subjects, is a significant decrease in the self-reported unpleasantness of painful stimuli and a correlated reduction in neural activity in brain areas known to be associated with affective and cognitive aspects of pain."[38]

In the study I joined, the sensory intensity ratings were the same for the controls and the meditators, but the level of unpleasantness reported in all aspects of pain was substantially reduced for the meditators. The neuroscientist J. A. Grant observes: "Beginners cannot inhibit automatic appraisal of their experience and actively reappraise it within the framework of mindfulness, whereas more experienced practitioners may actually achieve something closer to no appraisal."[39] One notable discovery in these studies is that the reported reduction of unpleasantness occurred with the practice of open monitoring (open awareness) and not with referential meditation. Hence the importance of open awareness in preparing us for reverse meditation.

Another significant discovery has been that meditators showed an *increase* in neural activity in areas associated with the sensory aspect of pain, which supports our claim that with these practices you feel things more, but they hurt you less. Seasoned meditators learn how to decouple the sensory input from affective and cognitive proliferation, preventing simple sensory data from ballooning into emotional and conceptual suffering. Thompson summarizes: "The meditator cultivates an open, stable, and nonselective awareness that disengages from the dualistic phenomenal framework of subject and object along with the approach-versus-avoid framework of seeing to obtain the desirable and avoid the undesirable."[40]

With science and spirituality on our side, it's time to jump into some pain—and learn how not to jump out.

CHAPTER 11

REVERSE MEDITATION
IN FOUR STEPS

The purpose of this practice is to transform our
experience of pain, and therefore to also transform
the mental suffering that accompanies it.

—DZOGCHEN PONLOP

The time has come to recognize that negative circumstances
can be transformed into spiritual power and attainment. . . .
Utilize adversities and obstacles as the path!

—PADMASAMBHAVA

On this road less traveled, "slow and easy" rules the day. Listen to
your heart as you proceed into the following instructions, and
trust your *inner* voice. Don't listen to the superficial chatter that tells
you that you can't do it. Listen to the voice that whispers the truth
that you can.

AS YOU START

A preliminary step. Returning to the instructions in chapter 7, start with a few minutes of referential shamatha to settle your mind. When you feel centered, transition into the practice of open awareness, and connect to the quality of space.

How long you do these preliminaries is up to you—it takes an honest practitioner to know when they're settled and open. The reverse meditations follow a traditional tantric maxim: the preliminaries are more important than the main practice. Without a solid on-ramp, the force of your habitual aversion to pain kicks in, and that will kick you right out of these meditations.

After you've established the space of "I don't mind what happens," you can now apply it in the four steps that follow. This doesn't mean you have to perfect the preliminaries before you step into the reverse meditations, but that you understand the principles. The reverse meditations work in a bidirectional way with the practice of open awareness (and the other preliminary practices). Open awareness feeds forward to provide the room to engage in the reverse meditations, while the reverse meditations feed back to reinforce open awareness. In other words, "I don't mind what happens" is both tested and strengthened by the reverse meditations. As Nietzsche said, "That which does not kill me only makes me stronger." Although a bit extreme, you get the idea. And remember, nothing is stronger than space.

STEP 1

Observe: briefly pull back from the pain and witness it. First, do something that hurts. For the next few minutes, dig your fingernail into your thumb or gently bite your tongue or lip. If you're already in discomfort, work with that. Those who feel tempted to really chomp down on themselves may want to take a look at that.[1] We're not trying to create meditative masochists. On a scale of 1 to 10, with level 1 being uncomfortable and 10 being unbearable, start with level 1 or 2. Once you get the hang of it, you can ramp it up. If you start with an experience that is too intense, the power of your habitual patterns (even survival-level instincts) will steamroll over the meditation. Notice what you feel in the rest of your body when you initiate the pain. Do you notice a contraction, or physical recoiling? Don't judge, just observe. If you feel an initial contraction, open up to that. Almost like Lamaze breathing, breathe into and ventilate both the contraction and the pain that ignited the contraction.

After witnessing the pain for a few minutes, drop everything. Return to body and breath. Open and relax. Short sessions, repeated often, are key to this practice. When you've caught your breath, you can either return to do this first step again or proceed to the following steps. I recommend pausing between each of the four steps, then repeating each step until you get the hang of it. If you proceed into all four steps right away, it can be too much to integrate. Go slow. This is unfamiliar territory.

Step 1 is to observe the unwanted experience and to briefly differentiate from it. You step back before you step in. Mingyur Rinpoche describes how dealing with intense physical pain enabled him "to get some distance between myself and my unease. My expanded sense of self grew bigger than the problem. It was able to accommodate the negative reaction to sound within a larger sphere, so that I was no longer the exact size and shape of my discomfort. The unease was still there. It didn't disappear, but I was no longer trapped inside it."[2]

The trick is to avoid stepping all the way out—be careful of slipping into the near enemy of dissociation.[3] Step 1 involves temporarily distancing yourself from the experience to get a better view of it. The philosopher Sam Harris writes, "That which is aware of sadness is not sad. That which is aware of fear is not fearful."[4] That which is aware of pain is not pained. Or as the medieval theologian Thomas Aquinas put it, "Whatever knows certain things cannot have any of them in its own nature."

The first step is to also catch the impulse to run away from the pain and to avoid getting swept up in the commentary that serves to distract you from the pain. You want to cultivate a witness awareness. The idea is to ride the impulse to get away from the unwanted experience—not to escape from it, but to get a better bead on it. Ken Wilber writes:

> To the extent that you actually realize that you are not, for example, your anxieties [or pain], then your anxieties no longer threaten you. Even if anxiety is present, it no longer overwhelms you because you are no longer exclusively tied to it. You are no longer courting it, fighting it, resisting it, or running from it. In the most radical fashion, anxiety is thoroughly accepted as it is and allowed to move as it will. You have nothing to lose, nothing to gain, by its presence or absence, for you are simply watching it pass by. . . . Thus, your personal mind-and-body may be in pain, or humiliation, or fear, but as long as you abide as the witness of these affairs, as if from on high, they no longer threaten you, and thus you are no longer moved to manipulate them, wrestle with them, or subdue them. Because you are willing to witness them, to look at them impartially, you are able to transcend them. . . . Likewise, if we can but watch or witness our distresses, we prove

ourselves thereby to be "distress-less," free of the witnessed turmoil. That which feels pain is itself pain-less; that which feels fear is fear-less; that which perceives tension is tensionless. To witness these states is to transcend them. They no longer seize you from behind because you look at them up front.[5]

Some people find that this step is enough. It's as far as they want to go. Because the witness is removed from the pain, this first step is easier to handle. If this is you, that's perfectly fine. Don't feel that you have to go into the next steps. But for the deeper divers, there's a further plunge.

STEP 2

Be with the pain, without running commentary on it. A limitation of step 1 is that it can slide into distraction, a pulling apart from the experience. The first step is still dualistic: I am witnessing the pain. Pain only becomes spiritual when it becomes nondualistic.

For step 2, reinitiate the pain, witness it briefly, then pull a U-turn and go directly into it. Be with it. Reverse your conditioned response to avoid the pain. This isn't easy, because it goes against the forces of both nature and nurture. Despite the maxim "not too tight, not too loose," you want to be too loose with this second step. Titrate the experience: continuously measure and adjust the balance of what you can manage. You can work up to longer sessions and more intense discomfort, but for now keep it short . . . and sour.

Observing the pain in step 1 begins to transform it. With step 2, you start to engage it, but without the usual conceptual proliferation (prapañca) that accompanies unwanted experience. Notice the tendency to run from the pain, and into commentary about it. "Man, this is stupid," or "Why am I doing this?" or "Am I doing this right?" The practice is to "catch and release." Catch that avoidant tendency, then release it. Drop back down into your body and stay with the pain.

Being with the pain also acts as a segue into step 3, which is examining the pain. In other words, being with it in step 2 invites a somatic exploration of pain, instead of merely an observational one, as in step 1. Step 2 is about facing the unwanted experience directly, which means feeling it. It's a visceral "meet and greet." Transformation really begins at the level of feeling. It takes guts, because until you get close enough, you have to be willing to take some hits. Tsoknyi Rinpoche offers the image of two boxers, who can knock the beans out of each other if they have enough room to throw their punches. But if you've ever watched a boxing match, you've seen that the fighters will occasionally get tangled together, so close to each other that there isn't room to throw a punch. The best they can do is dole out a few baby punches, which amount to nothing more than some taps on the sides of the rib cage. This is the spirit of step 2: being so close to the unwanted experience that it no longer packs a punch.

Do you remember Ajahn Chah's advice to the young monk who was complaining about all the noise? "The sound isn't bothering you; you are bothering the sound." The practice at step 2 is to not bother the unwanted feeling. Then, armed with your view of sacred outlook, you can start to trust what you're feeling, seeing the basic goodness within it. But don't expect anything. Expectation is premeditated disappointment. Just be with the feeling; stay open to whatever arises. Don't expect to feel good. Just be real. Our goal in the reverse meditations is to alleviate suffering, but the journey is the goal. If your goals and expectations are too rigid, it will sabotage the practice.

You can see that while the steps proceed in a linear fashion, they also interpenetrate, informing and supporting each other. The examination of step 3 leaks back to inform your practice of step 2. With some experience in all four steps, you'll discover how they all cross-pollinate and bootstrap each other. Don't tie yourself into knots trying to do every step precisely and perfectly. Get a feel for it. Find your own way in. All four steps are there to support you in staying with the pain and to help you go into it as deeply as you can.

STEP 2 (CONTINUED)

After being with the pain for a few minutes, drop everything. Catch your breath. Notice any commentary, but without judgment.

If you choose to practice all four steps of the reverse meditations, you'll eventually be able to cascade through all of them in a single session, but until you get the gist of things, take this one step at a time. Stay with steps 1 and 2 until you're familiar with them. You'll make many discoveries just by doing these two steps, and this may be enough for you.

THE END OF HABIT

In both Hinduism and Buddhism, staying in the fires of experience is the way to purify our bad habits, especially the relentless habit of contraction. In Eastern language, it's the way to purify karma. Remember Suzuki Roshi, "You should burn yourself completely. If you do not burn yourself completely, a trace of yourself will be left in what you do." People are rightly concerned about the importance of not leaving a carbon footprint. Being fully with difficult experiences (step 2), cremating them as you live them, leaves no *karmic* footprint. As the iconoclastic teacher Da Free John liked to say, "The fire must have its way." If you don't stay in the fire, a footprint is left in the unconscious mind and conditions the way you'll relate to similar experiences in the future.

"When any experience is resisted, it does not dissolve completely, but leaves behind a trace of itself called a *samskāra*, which literally means 'impression,'" Christopher Wallis writes.

> Whenever we turn away, even partially, from what is happening in the present moment because it is too uncomfortable, too painful, or even too wonderful, it creates a *samskāra*. When we resist reality, don't show up, go unconscious, or "check out," then we don't fully receive the experience, we don't allow it to fully pass through our being, and that is why it leaves an impression.[6]

In popular parlance, "what we resist persists." These unfinished energy patterns, or undigested experiences, born of our bad habit of contracting against them, then manifest as reactions (contractions) disproportionate to what's actually happening. Our buttons are being pressed (buttons that we've unwittingly installed), because we're reacting to what's present *and* to the undigested past experiences. We often react *more* to the past than to the present (as in the line from James Joyce: "History is a nightmare from which I am trying to awake"). To resolve the past impression, and prevent new ones from being deposited, we need to follow the exhortation of the philosopher Kṣemarāja and "become one with the Fire of Consciousness."

In other words, you need to let go of all the secondary and tertiary conceptual contractions and stay fully with the unwanted experience. The samskāras are karmic triggers. When they're present, reactivity (instead of response-ability) and karma are created. If you are completely open to what you're feeling, a capacity cultivated in step 2, you devour the experience and leave no karmic footprint behind. Wallis writes: "Let your attitude be one of wonder and curiosity: 'Wow! My mind is totally freaking out right now! That's amazing! I wonder why it's reacting so strongly when everything's actually okay?'" He advises, "You can learn to watch the energy"—as in step 1 of the reverse meditations—"surging up inside and the stories the mind tells about it, without believing or disbelieving them, but being curious about where it's all coming from"[7]—as in step 3 of the reverse meditations.

Because you're ending karma, you're also ending "rebirth." You're stopping the process of *involuntary* entry into unwanted states of mind. You can still take *voluntary* rebirth into healthy states of mind, no longer driven by habitual self-centered and contracting impulses, but driven by openness, expressed as love and compassion. The primordial contraction that gave birth to the self, the worst of all habits, is replaced with the openness that gives birth to selflessness. From that centerless stance, you spontaneously express your selfless love in the service of others.

STEP 3

Examine: investigate the nature of pain. Step 3 is to examine the pain. Bring analytic meditation into the picture. Look deeply into the nature of your pain. Be curious. What is pain? What is it made of? Look. Find out for yourself. What exactly is this thing that I have spent so much of my life trying to avoid?

This step brings concepts back into the scene, but these are healthy concepts in the form of questions that send the mind in the right direction. The conceptual proliferation of prapañca pulls the mind away; this analytic step invites the conceptual mind back in. Khenpo Karthar Rinpoche says, "If we are experiencing intense physical pain and if we look directly at the essence, nature of the experience, this will not get rid of it, but it will no longer be intolerable. This is because we will then be in the midst of it rather than viewing it from the outside. In this way, the practice finally consists of resting directly in whatever arises."[8]

This investigation shows you that what you call pain and suffering are constructs, and can therefore be deconstructed. It's part of our "divide and conquer" strategy. When you're in pain, there's obviously something there. But it's not what you think it is. By using directed concepts in the form of inquiries to cut through proliferating concepts (your storylines about what you think pain is), you can deconstruct your usual narratives and reduce this thing called pain to its fundamental constituents. This step often appeals to intellectuals, academics, and scientists, who can now engage the incisive mind to take pain apart.

STEP 3 (CONTINUED)

Expanding on traditional analytic meditation, you can ask, "Does this pain have a color, a shape, a texture? Where, precisely, is this pain coming from? Is there something within, or underneath, this pain?" And my favorite question: "Who is feeling this pain?" This last query flips the investigation from the feeling to the feeler and acts as a segue into step 4. Can you find the experiencer of this experience? When taken to heart, this question is a game changer.

These investigations do not dismiss the phenomenon we label "pain," but they do dismiss all the adventitious defilements, the storylines, the constructs, that we immediately plaster onto this sensation. These investigations lead to the discovery that pain is just intense sensory awareness. And below even that: pain is just naked awareness itself (a topic we'll unpack below). Don't take my word on it. Look. Find out for yourself.

STEP 3 (CONTINUED)

After a minute or two of examining your pain, let everything go. Rest for as long as it takes to catch your breath. Notice the cascade of thoughts and emotions that often arise right after doing the reverse meditation. It's common for the mind to scramble as you struggle to become familiar with the unfamiliar, to wrap your mind around something so different. "Am I doing this right? I'm not so sure about this practice! Did I miss something? This is ridiculous!" A sense of levity goes a long way in this step. You're trying to lighten up, and touching into the initial absurdity of the reverse meditations helps. With time, the absurdity is replaced with profundity.

Then repeat. Bite your lip, dig your fingernail into your thumb, do something that hurts. Go gently but fearlessly into the discomfort. Feel into the contraction, or your initial reaction to the pain. Do you notice how the contraction, which is your resistance, exacerbates the pain? The equation "suffering equals pain times resistance" comes back into play.

In step 3, your underlying resistance is being brought into the light of consciousness, where you can now relate to it. The core contraction is revealed to be your default reaction to pain. Contraction is how the non-meditative mind holds—or in this case, squeezes—the experience. This conventional crucible, the big squeeze, does not transform lead into gold. It transforms gold into lead. It transforms pain, intense sensory awareness, into suffering. By uncovering this core contraction, you can gradually replace it with expansion. By transforming the crucible, or holding environment, you transform the pain.

Remember that the ultimate holding environment is space. The crucible of a spacious mind, nurtured with open awareness, comes back to gently, but indestructibly, hold your pain. The open mind is fireproof, bulletproof, not because it's impenetrable, but because there is absolutely no-thing to penetrate.

STEP 4

Yoke with the pain: become one with it. The final step is to drop any level of investigation and dissolve fully into the pain. In meditative terms, yoke or unite with the pain. The reverse meditations finally become a true yoga with this last step. How is this different from step 2? In step 2 you were invited to be with the pain; in step 4 you're invited to be the pain.

This radical step purifies the pain—that is, it purifies any level of contraction away from it, or conceptuality about it. It empties the pain. By removing any concepts, you're emptying it of inherent existence. You're fully deconstructing and therefore dereifying the pain—transforming a thing into a no-thing. This leads to the liberating discovery that *if you become one with your pain, there is no one to hurt.*

What's left? Nothing but pure sensory awareness, however intense it may be, that you stain with the label "pain." What's left is sensation, stripped of a lifetime of adverse conditioning, disrobed of all your projections and imputations, purified of the hope of never having to feel pain again and the fear that you will. You finally see pain for what it really is, and dis-cover that this emperor that rules your life really has no clothes. Pain is revealed to be nothing but raw, unadulterated, pure sensory awareness. That's it. Now it's legit. You discover the truth of the idea that suffering is a ready substitute for legitimate pain. Stay with the legitimate experiential intensity, and you'll not only remove all your suffering, you'll also get rid of your pain. "By going more deeply into our experience of suffering, we open up the inner light of spaciousness and love within it," writes Zvi Ish-Shalom. "At the heart of every contraction is the vast light of Being, of deep and profound peace."[9]

The word *peace* is derived from a proto-Indian-European root that means "to fasten" or "a binding together." When you fasten yourself to the present moment (with referential shamatha), and open yourself to the intensity of what is happening (with open awareness and the reverse meditations), you can discover peace tucked within your pain. The way to do this is to stay fully embodied, in complete contact with the physical sensation. In the Canki Sutta the Buddha taught that supreme truth is realized with the body. As T. S. Eliot wrote, "Music heard so deeply that it is not heard at all, but you are the music while the music lasts." Pain felt so deeply and purely that it is not felt at all—in the conventional way.

When you contract away from pain in self-defense, you're actually contracting onto nothing. It seems like you're contracting back to yourself, referring the experience back to central headquarters, which results in the assumption that "I'm feeling this pain." But that's not what's happening. Yes, your body is registering the pain, but is that who you really are? If it's "my" body, it can't be me. What's really happening is that the contraction itself creates the illusion that there is a self, an experiencer, someone to hurt. This leads to the revelation that *self = contraction.*

Your very sense of self, once again, is nothing more than a primordial contraction, which becomes heightened when the contraction is heightened. Isn't it true that you never feel more solid and real than when you're in pain? You can therefore use this heightening as a way to better explore not just the pain, but the self that seems to be experiencing it. When we contract, pain is brought into existence, along with the reified sense of self that experiences it (topics we'll unfold in chapter 13).

STEP 4 (CONTINUED)

Let's return to the actual practice and conclude the instruction. Before you end your session, heighten the pain before you let it go. Take it briefly up to a level 5 or 6. Then drop everything and relax.

The postscript inquiry is this: Do you prefer one state over the other? Of course you do. Only a masochist would think otherwise. But as outrageous as it seems, the meditation masters do not. Milarepa said, "When pleasure and pain are not two different things, this is [meditation] instruction as mastered as it can be." And Trunpga Rinpoche wrote of pleasure and pain that "become ornaments which it is pleasant to wear." Practitioners at this level have no preference for samsāra or nirvāṇa. They have achieved nonduality.

THE STEPS IN REVIEW

The reverse meditations represent four steps, or stages, in establishing a nondual relationship to pain. Step 1 is to briefly pull back from the pain and observe it. Step 2 is to be with the pain without running commentary on it. Step 3 is to examine the nature of pain. Step 4 is to yoke with the pain—to become one with it. The acronym OBEY can be a way to remember the four steps: Observe the pain; then Be with it; then Examine it; finally, Yoke or unite with it.

The nuance between steps 2 and 4, once again, is that step 2 asks you to descend from the witnessing first step and be *with* the pain. It's still dualistic. Step 4 is to *be* the pain. The witness dissolves into that being witnessed—the experience has become nondual. And by deconstructing the experience of pain, you're simultaneously deconstructing the experiencer of the pain. Self and other go up in smoke. You're finally a good bonfire, cremating your experience as you live it.

In chapter 2, words from Trungpa Rinpoche offered insight about discovering the sacred in the profane, and they are worth revisiting now that you've gained a more refined understanding of what it means to have a nondual relationship to unwanted experiences:

> We could say that the real world is that in which we experience pleasure and pain, good and bad. . . . *But if we are completely in touch with these dualistic feelings, that absolute experience of duality is itself the experience of non-duality.* Then there is no problem at all, because duality [pain] is seen from a perfectly open and clear point of view in which there is no conflict; there is a tremendous encompassing vision of oneness. Conflict arises because duality [pain] is not seen as it is at all. It [pain] is only seen in a biased way, a very clumsy way.[10]

The reverse meditations put us completely in touch with painful/dualistic feelings, and that absolute experience of duality/pain is then discovered to be the experience of nonduality. When they're experienced fully, contractions transform into expansions. This reveals the utter immediacy of nonduality, and at the same time reveals how we create duality moment to moment by not experiencing things fully. The reverse meditations create this contact with absolute reality because they show us how to properly touch, and stay in touch, with what was previously too hot to handle. The British scientist John Wren-Lewis said, "The ill comes when one is not fully conscious of something. It's the limitation of consciousness that causes it to be painful."[11]

By getting so completely in touch with pain (or anything else) that you become one with it, you experience the "tremendous encompassing vision of oneness." The Buddhist scholar Ngawang Zangpo puts it another way: "Tantra is contact spirituality (as in contact sport)."[12] By making deep contact with your feelings, you're making contact with nonduality.

Although a nondual relationship to pain can be established in the step-by-step process of the reverse meditations, with some familiarity you may find yourself skipping steps, going back and forth between them, or mixing them together. The four steps amount to four options for how to work with unwanted experience. Stick with just one, or explore in whatever combinations you like. See what works best for you.

Some practitioners associate each of the four steps with a corresponding somatic sensation. One person in a retreat I hosted reported that when she's observing the unwanted experience, she feels a strong movement of energy coming up her spine and lifting out of her crown. Observing and examining generated an upward movement into spirit; while being with it and yoking generated downward movements into matter, the body: ascending and descending currents, alternating with each of the four steps. Another participant shared a similar comment,

> "Observe" and "Examine" feel energetically similar, like parallel vibrations an octave apart. "Examine," the higher vibration, holds a sense of more clarity, even purity, than "Observation." "Examine" becomes a witness to the witness, a meta-witnessing, that's first developed in "Observe" as the witness. So, meta-witnessing feels natural during examination. But both are reaching upwards for higher consciousness, for a longer view of things. For me, the stages of "Be with it" and "Yoke," have a pulling down into the body effect. "Be with it" and "Yoking" are physical! "Be with it" has an overall sinking into the lower chakras for me—a literal sense of sinking into the earth, becoming part of the ground. But it's still not all the way. For full embodiment to be accomplished, the "Yoke," the utter union, must be accomplished. The "Yoke" of Body-Heart-Mind is where it all comes together. The Union leads to the embodying of pain as Pure Perception. Though there is still awareness of the pain, it no longer contains painful suffering.

Another person discovered that taking the unwanted experience to the level of absurdity brought a sense of levity: "I wanted to see what would happen if I took this unwanted state of mind as far as possible. It was almost like blowing up a balloon—how big could I make it? Then something happened: it popped! And so did I! I burst out laughing."

"UNFAMILIAR TO MYSELF"

The meditation master Mingyur Rinpoche engaged in a four-year reverse meditation when he left his palatial life as a high-ranking Tibetan lama and set out alone on the rugged streets of India to embark on the life of a wandering yogi. Early in his journey, he boarded one of those overcrowded Indian trains and reflected, "I could have traveled first class, and waited in the lounge with the ceiling fans. But this is what I asked for . . . circumstances so unfamiliar as to make me unfamiliar to myself."[13] That's what you're doing with the reverse meditations. Putting yourself in situations so unfamiliar that you're forced to expand to accommodate the new experience.

Remember that the Tibetan word for meditation (*gom*) means "to become familiar with." The reverse meditations propel you into *unfamiliar*, and uncomfortable, territory. You need to be kind and patient to yourself as you stretch into this new terrain. The problem with pain (or any other unwanted experience) is not pain itself, but the fact that you're so unfamiliar with it, and that you experience it in a partial and therefore dualistic way. You have probably never given yourself the chance to get to know it, and befriend it. Even if you're living with the harrowing challenges of chronic pain, the question still remains: have you ever taken the time to get to know your pain? Or are you so involved in trying to avoid it that you don't really know the enemy?

Becoming familiar with your adversary is the art of war, from the Chinese tradition, or greater jihad, from esoteric Islam.[14] How do you properly go into battle against pain? What kind of armor do you need? The armor of understanding. Marie Curie famously said, "Nothing in life is to be feared. It is only to be understood." In the nondual terms of meditation, Christopher Wallis says more about the need for understanding: "Most of what is unpleasant about human existence is not pain, but mind-created suffering. And we can be free of this suffering, for the Tantric scriptures tell us it is entirely a product of ignorance, of *not seeing things as they really are*."[15]

You don't need to become a spiritual martyr and always grind it out when you're in pain. But if you bother to spend time with your pain, and really understand it, you might surprise yourself with your ability to manage it in a new way. The capacity of the open mind to accommodate any unwanted experience is a revelation for those willing to do the inner work. The biologist Bruce Lipton writes, "Harnessing the power of your mind can be *more* effective than the drugs you have been programmed to believe you need."[16]

Nobody knows how they're going to react when they undertake the eccentric approach of reverse meditation. That's part of the practice. Give yourself time to explore these uncharted waters, with an attitude of openness, curiosity, and radical kindness to yourself.

CHAPTER 12

REVERSE MEDITATION
IN DAILY LIFE

Easy, comfortable practice won't get you anywhere!

—MILAREPA

Don't try to avoid hardship, but accept whatever comes.

—CHATRAL RINPOCHE

The power of the reverse meditations came home to me about fifteen years ago. I was living alone at the time, and in the dead of one transformative night, I woke up abruptly with a stabbing pain in my side. I started to palpate the area, mentally cascading through a host of differential diagnoses: "Appendicitis? Intercostal muscle cramp? Intestinal blockage?" When I tapped the area with my hand, I about went through the roof and made the immediate diagnosis: kidney stones.

I got out of bed to head to the medicine cabinet and buckled over because of the intensity of the pain. It was 3:00 am, and I debated whether I should rush to the emergency room. But my memory of pathology from dental school informed me that short of narcotic-level analgesics, lithotripsy (breaking up the stone with ultrasound), or emergency surgery (which wasn't going to happen in the middle of the night), I'd probably end up sitting in a cold waiting room all night waiting for the urologist to show up in the morning.

I took 800 mg of ibuprofen and went downstairs to my shrine room, where I had practiced the reverse meditations for years. Now it was time to perform. I was in too much pain to sit upright, so I curled into a ball on the floor, went directly into the pain, and said, "Okay, take me!" It took a few excruciating minutes to surrender to it. I would dip into the pain, but it was so fierce that I'd reflexively pull out. Like slowly submerging into ice-cold water, I worked my way in and took the plunge. Then to my delight, there really was no one left to hurt! The "pain" was gone. What remained is hard to put into words. It was very intense sensory awareness that, in the strangest way, transformed into a type of bliss. This was far from your garden-variety bliss. It did not feel good. But the point is this: it also did not feel bad. What I was left with felt super real, but paradoxically it did not feel solid.

I later realized that what I had experienced was "enlightened pain," or the purified pain of step 4 of the reverse meditations. Pain that was no longer encumbered by all my hopes and fears, my historical conditioning, my stern resistance—all of which generate "endarkened," or normal, pain. Instead of screaming out "NO!" to what I was feeling, I whispered an indestructible "Yes!" I had "lightened up" in the most ineffable way, and what I previously knew as pain lifted away. The experience was still there, in all its raging intensity, but my relationship to it was profoundly transformed.

Years later I came across this statement from David Loy: "Many of the classical Zen stories tell of students being enlightened by [intense] actions. What happens in such cases is that the shock of the unexpected noise or pain penetrates to the very core of the student's being—that is, it is experienced nondually. When Yün-men broke his ankle, he was enlightened because he forgot himself and everything else as his universe collapsed into one excruciating but empty pain."[1] That was it! The sensation I'd had that night in the shrine room was so full, yet inexpressibly empty.

As I was lying on the floor, that line from Milarepa had been running through my head: "The suffering being bliss feels so good that feeling bad feels good."[2] I was experiencing the yogic joy Milarepa sang about, a type of joy available to any yogi or yogini who is willing to accept the invitation to relate to pain in this outrageous way and obey (that is, OBEY) the inner command to open.

I spent the rest of that night in this state of "bliss," then promptly went to see my doctor in the morning. He did an ultrasound, immediately located the stones, told me surgery would not be necessary, and that like all things this too would "pass." The doctor gave me a prescription for sixty Percocet (!), which I filled just in case, but I didn't take a single pill. Norman Cousins, author of the landmark book *Anatomy of an Illness* says, "The human mind is a remarkable apothecary,"[3] and indeed, since my experience dealing with kidney stones I have had dental work without anesthetic, several minor surgeries where no post-op analgesia was necessary, and countless other bumps and bruises, all managed with the pharmacy of my own mind.

The phenomenon of transforming obstacle into opportunity could not have been more dramatic. That single event continues to inspire me to share these unconventional meditations with others. Don't let anyone tell you that meditation, or spirituality, doesn't have real-world application. It is the ultimate painkiller.

Here's another example from quite recently. After a standard physical exam and routine tests, my primary care physician was concerned about the lab report and referred me to a urologist. The specialist ordered more tests. I went in for an MRI, which was preceded by the insertion of an IV (to inject a contrast dye), and a host of other quite objectionable procedures. (I'll spare you the gruesome details—lest you contract!) I can't say I looked forward to it, but neither did I look away. Armed with my confidence in the reverse meditations, I went in with the attitude, "Okay, let's make this a rich morning for practice," and reframed the event as an opportunity to work with my mind. As they placed me into the MRI for a forty-five-minute scan (which is incredibly loud, even with earplugs), I slid into my practice of reverse sound meditation (described below). Before the scan, when they were searching for a good vein for the IV, it took several stabs of the needle—and I slipped into the reverse pain meditation. One of the nurses remarked, "You are *not* our normal patient." The MRI came back with a suspicious lesion, which led to an even more invasive series of needle biopsies, which led to a less-than-ideal diagnosis: prostate cancer.[4]

The diagnosis did not freak me out. Of course, I wish I didn't have to go through the upcoming radical prostatectomy and all the other unpleasantries of major surgery, but I'm okay with it. I have not been walloped with such a serious diagnosis before, so I had to look closely at my equanimous response. Was I just repressing the bad news? Is there subliminal denial going on? I can't find anything of the sort. I can only share what I feel in my heart: I am not afraid. I know that when the surgeon cuts me open, nothing can cut into who I really am. Throughout the entire affair (which is in progress as I write these words), the reverse meditations have been a trusted friend at my side, helping me ride the experience without being thrown by it.

In my experience, along with others who have engaged these practices, it doesn't take much formal practice before you'll start to spontaneously "perform," before these meditations come to fruition on the stage of life. If you work with the reverse meditations even briefly, they will start to work with you. Perhaps the intensity of the practice downloads into your body-mind more quickly than other meditations. Perhaps the focus required to do the reverse meditations enables rapid incorporation. For whatever reason, when I have a leg cramp or get a paper cut, instead of the old "oh, crap!" reactivity, I now respond with "oh—practice!" Instead of contracting, I open. It doesn't even become "pain" until I leave my body and enter my concepts. Maybe you've had a glimpse of this experience when you stub your toe, feel the impact, but for a moment don't feel any pain. It takes a second for the sensation to be transmitted, and then registered, as pain.

When I have a headache, backache, or any other painful situation, I'm perfectly game to seek conventional ways of blunting the pain. I still take an analgesic when needed, and I go to appropriate healthcare professionals like anybody else. But I also apply these anti-inflammatory meditations to the pain, which keep me in literal touch with what's really happening in my body—and out of the incendiary conceptual processes that transform the inevitable sparks of life into infernos.

One of the most haunting images I have ever seen is the photograph of Thich Quang Duc, the Vietnamese monk, self-immolating in protest of religious persecution during the war. Here is a human being, sitting in meditative equipoise while his entire body is set ablaze. How is it humanly possible for anyone to do this? How on earth can someone sit unflinching as their body is consumed in flames? It's because fire cannot burn space. Who knows what this monk did, but perhaps he mixed his mind with space and opened to the fire. Perhaps he knew that if he became one with his pain, there would be no one to burn.

FEELING AND MANAGING EMOTIONS

The reverse meditations have gradually instilled a quality of physical and emotional indestructibility in my life. When I was living alone in the mountains, and my marriage was falling apart, I struggled with tremendous emotional pain. I felt the temptation to distract myself with entertainment, or dilute the anguish with alcohol, but elected to stay in the emotional furnace and work with my feelings.

Following the steps reflected in the acronym OBEY, I began by Observing the pain. Instead of relating *from* my heartache, I related *to* it. Simply watching it started to change it. Then I allowed myself to Be with the feelings. It took some guts to be with the fire, but staying with my feelings started to soften them. I felt them in a new way—more intimate, but less personal. I then took the next step and started to Examine what I was feeling. What exactly is this raw emotional pain? Where am I feeling it? What makes it feel so bad? And *who* is feeling it? Asking these questions sent me in the right direction—into the sensation instead of away from it.

I discovered that every time I contracted away from the heartache, I intensified it. Trying to escape only made it worse. By staying with it, and inquiring deeply, I started to transform my pain. By letting go of my storylines, letting go of all the history I stained the experience with, I purified the emotional pain by returning to what pain really is—raw awareness.

I then took the final step and dissolved fully (Yoked) into the feelings, becoming (n)one with them. By becoming one with them, "I" became "none." I disappeared into the feelings (or the feelings disappeared into me), which self-liberated the negativity of the feelings along with the feeler. As with my kidney stones, what I was left with did not feel good, but it also did not feel bad. It felt real, but not solid. It felt honest, and ineffably complete.

By going 100 percent into the feeling, I removed the flickers of reference, the super-fast contractions (the tachycardia of the ego), that generate the illusion that *I* am feeling the pain. Pain then becomes truly "selfless"—so it feels better. It's purified of the stain of self. Now when I feel emotional distress, I feel it as fully and cleanly as possible. I'll say to myself, "I'm going to feel this loneliness, this anxiety, this rejection, this worry, as completely as I can." Sometimes I'll put it in the form of a question, "I wonder what this sadness feels like if I feel it 100 percent?" I try to be a good bonfire. The trick is to avoid indulging the feeling, which I can always tell is happening because the storylines kick in. Whenever storylines appear, I release the commentary and return to the feeling.

Because I've done the reverse meditations for so long, I'll often go directly to step 4 and obey the command to dissolve into the feeling. If I'm really hurting, I might do this with my eyes closed, curled up underneath a blanket. But it's not a pity party. It's just my way of allowing myself to be fully human. (Before you can become a buddha, you have to become fully human. You may then discover that being fully human *is* to become a buddha.)

I've also discovered that if the emotional energy is brief, like an overreaction to something, the energy can't stand up to any of the steps of the reverse meditation; it dissolves on contact. If I try to be it 100 percent, the outburst just melts and self-liberates. On a recent morning a friend sent me an email that I thought was careless. It zinged me. I felt my irritation and noticed it starting to build into anger. So I closed my eyes, dropped the developing storylines, and felt into the irritation as fully as possible. It evaporated. But then I reread the email an hour later and got irritated once more. This time, out of curiosity, I let the energy build (by indulging my storylines). The irritation grew into an emotional bully, getting stronger and more solid the more I capitulated to my saucy stories. It started to push me around. After a few minutes, I turned to face the bully square in the eye, calling its bluff (by dropping my storylines), and it withered away like the Wicked Witch of the West.

I'm not trying to smack down every unwanted emotion that pops up, as if I'm playing Whac-A-Mole. I allow the space for anything to arise, and I feel things like anybody else. But it does amount to a type of stare down. Not in a repressive way, but in a curious and analytic way. I stare directly into the unwanted feeling and reduce it *down* to its energetic essence, instead of letting it build *up* into an emotional thug. It's important to avoid having any expectations as I do this; the point is to face the emotion head-on, welcome it but not indulge it, and then see what happens. Reverse meditation practice doesn't whitewash your expressive life, leaving you emotionally barren. Your feelings are still there, but now they're purified (dereified) emotions. You feel them as never before, but you feel them as clean energy that burns purely—leaving no trace.

In all of its many beneficial applications, reverse meditation has had the greatest impact on my emotional life. Until I engaged these practices, I held the impression that as a spiritual practitioner I needed to be more chill. When I got swept up in an emotion, I felt like a bad meditator. The reverse meditations have shown me that I don't need to artificially chill out. I just need to know how to properly turn on the flames.

Earlier in my practice, when I was only doing mindfulness meditation, every time I drifted into an emotion and away from my referent (body, breath, candle, mantra), I felt like I was failing. Feeling an emotion fully was inappropriate with referential meditation. But in the spirit of "transcend but include," the reverse meditations engage my ability to stay fully present in an appropriate way—not with my breath (or other referent) but instead with a difficult feeling, or state of mind.

Let's say I'm starting a meditation session in a foul mood, or I'm in a foul mood and decide to meditate upon that state of mind. Because of that emotional state, I'll elect to practice the reverse meditations instead of a referential practice. Instead of trying to stay with my breath, as I would if I were doing a referential practice, I now stay as fully as I can with that foul state of mind. The practice becomes noticing all the static, how my ego doesn't want to feel so foul.

I often do this practice with my hand over my heart, which reminds me I'm okay just the way I am, no matter how screwed up I feel. I'm not just okay. I'm divine. And the energy coursing through my body is perfect—if I just feel it perfectly. If I can be completely present with what I'm feeling right now, even when I feel like crap, that's perfection. It's a total acceptance of my human condition.

❀ INSTRUCTION

Try it yourself. Tune in to whatever you're feeling right now. It doesn't matter what it is: tune into it fully. Don't change a thing. If you're not feeling anything, feel that. Don't try to return to some silence or stillness (or your breath, your mantra, or whatever), which implies that somehow silence and stillness are superior to your current state of mind. Don't try to be spiritual. Be human. If you're 100 percent present with whatever you're experiencing, you'll find silence and stillness there. The only thing you want to silence is your protest against the way things are. If you're feeling like total shit, feel it fully. Your state of mind, right now, is complete and perfect just the way it is. There's no such thing as an underdeveloped moment. Nothing is missing—if you don't go missing.

You'll notice the static when your storylines kick in, and ego tries to tune out. Don't judge that. Let it come, then let it go. (Ironically, in my experience, the worse I feel, or the more intense the emotion, the easier this is to practice.)

This practice allows you to cremate your experience as you live it, and fully digest and metabolize your life so it doesn't leave a trace. In Sanskrit this assimilation of emotional energy is called haṭha-pāka, or "sudden digestion."* Christopher Wallis writes that, when this energy becomes activated,

> if we are able to hold it gently, seeing that it is nothing but another form of the same divine Awareness that manifests as all things, then that energy is suddenly "digested" rather than simply getting buried again. . . . To digest the energy, you need to let go of the storylines associated with it . . . release it so that you can be intimate with the feeling [itself]. . . . Access the underlying energy; that is what we want to digest.[5]

Most people can't metabolize experience in this way, resulting in various forms of experiential indigestion. From there, they react inappropriately to future situations, because they end up reacting

---

* In the bardo teachings of Tibetan Buddhism, consuming emotional energy so completely is what it means to "meet the deity." The Tibetans say that after you die, when all your contractions and conceptual proliferations are finally put to rest, you will encounter the hundred peaceful and wrathful deities. The deities represent purity—in other words, the experience of encountering a state of mind without reference point, experience without an experiencer. The deities are generated when the white light of Ein Sof (or dharmata in Buddhist terms) is refracted through a prism into five colored lights—a primordial palate of energy from which every other colorful emotion is comprised. By returning to these five lights (the emotional energies of purified passion, aggression, indifference, jealousy, pride) when you die, you turn into the five central meditation deities, which in turn spawn the hundred peaceful and wrathful deities.

But you don't have to wait till you die to meet these five deities. Just die to all your contractions, become (n)one with those emotions in life, and you will meet your emotional maker now. You will light up as never before. Anger then burns purely and turns into the deity Akshobhya, pride flames up and transforms into Ratnasambhava, passion ignites and turns into Amitabha, envy flares up and transforms into Amoghasiddhi, and indifference alights and turns into Vairochana. You don't actually meet these deities: you become them.

more to what they haven't previously digested than to what is actually happening. Their ability to properly respond goes out the window.

ADJUSTING THE VOLUME

The more you work with different applications of the reverse meditations, the more they support each other. The following practice uses the meditations to work with contractions created by noise, or any other form of chaos and cacophony.

✳ INSTRUCTION

Establish the preliminaries as before, with a few minutes of mindfulness and open awareness. Once you're settled, turn on your sound system, tune in to some noise (perhaps in the form of static), and crank it up. If you live in a big city, open the windows. The idea is to create, or step into, an environment that is loud enough to irritate you, but not loud enough to hurt your ears.

Notice how your body contracts when you're assaulted with noise. Open to that assault. A thought to keep in mind is that "when the mind gets big, problems get small; when the mind gets small, problems get big." Then repeat steps 1 through 4 of the reverse meditation practice, staying fully present with the noise: (1) observe the noise for a few minutes; (2) be with the noise without commentary; (3) examine it to penetrate its nature; (4) dissolve into it and unite with it. You're trying to OBEY a new order of relationship to unwanted stimuli. After several minutes, turn the sound off, step away from the chaos, and rest in silence and stillness. Notice what you feel. Does your body relax and open? Is your conceptual mind spinning with commentary? Do you prefer the silence over the noise? Once you've caught your breath, repeat the auditory insult. Can you find the silence in the noise? If you're working with a dissonant situation, can you find the stillness in the motion? Is the noise bothering you, or are you bothering the noise? Parents with boisterous children tell me that this meditation mimics their daily life, and therefore equips them to manage their crazy lives.

The practice is to remain unmoved in the center of this sonic cyclone. Notice the tendency to complain. Hold your seat. As with every reverse meditation, sustain your inquisitive attitude. David Loy writes, "In the Taoist doctrine of wu-wei, the cryptic teachings on 'not-doing,' one cultivates a silent center that does not move while activity constantly moves all around you. Chuang-tzu refers to it as 'tranquility-in-disturbance.'"[6] Loy adds, "Enlightenment occurs in Buddhism when the usually automatized reflexivity of contraction ceases, experienced as a letting go."[7]

When an ambulance, police car, or fire truck screams by, instead of wincing in self-defense, you may find yourself opening to the siren. When you go to Times Square, a raucous bus station, or any other frenzied place, instead of closing down from the assault, you'll relax into it. What previously interrupted your meditation now nurtures it.

THINK MORE

I learned the reverse meditations with this final example, which comes from the classic meditation manuals. It's a total twist on standard meditation.

🌸INSTRUCTION

Start as before, with a few minutes of mindfulness and open awareness. When you feel settled, do the opposite of what you normally do in meditation: create as many thoughts as possible. Let your mind go crazy. Think as many thoughts as you can, as fast as you can. How many thoughts, images, ruminations, and fantasies can you crank up? You finally have a meditation that allows you to do what you've always wanted to do!

To really whip things up, dart your eyes around, and take rapid short breaths. I find that staying with step 1, the witness, is enough for this reverse meditation. (But you can play with the other steps, and see how they work for you.) For many people, it's exhausting to generate so many thoughts. Notice how you can create this maelstrom and remain silent in the eye of the hurricane.

This practice can also be used to relate to insomnia in a healthier way.[8] When you wake up in the middle of the night and your mind is racing, instead of getting wigged out by the display, celebrate it. Instead of the usual "Damn! Now I'm going to be exhausted all day tomorrow," say, "Wow! Look at the velocity of this whirlpool! It's amazing how many thoughts my mind can create!" This reverse relationship often has the effect of settling your mind. Witness the display, but without getting sucked into it. Insomnia gets worse when you wrestle with your mind. If you hug your mind, you may find the tantrum transforming into tranquility. It's a nocturnal version of learning how to love your mind.

Once you're sensitized to all the contractions in your life, you'll realize that the opportunities for reverse meditation are endless. Every single time you feel self-consciousness or self-righteousness, anger or aggression, fear or panic, complaint or criticism, reactivity or judgment, grasping or attachment, stress or tension, you'll be able to realize the gifts they present. Enfolded within each one is a super expander. "The most mundane experiences of life can be portals to the most sublime dimensions of reality," Zvi Ish-Shalom writes. "Because every experience contains within it the totality."[9]

The instant you contract, you reify the experience and the experiencer. To reify is to solidify, to make more real. But the reverse meditations alter your relationship to pain and show you that your suffering increases in direct proportion to your levels of reification. The more you contract, the heavier *you* make the situation, and the more that gets you down. The reverse meditations reveal your role, and therefore your responsibility, in your happiness and your suffering. Are you willing to assume that responsibility?

CHAPTER 13

FINAL THOUGHTS

Emptiness, Nonduality, and the Reverse Meditations

To forget oneself and become one with something is at the same time to realize its emptiness and "transcend" it.

—DAVID R. LOY

The true value of a human being is determined primarily by the measure and the sense in which he has attained liberation from the self.

—ALBERT EINSTEIN

The meditations you've encountered in this book are enough to alter your relationship to pain, but the material in this final chapter is meant to help you plumb the depths of these practices. You have seen how the reverse meditations undo the lightning-fast construction project, managed by the ego as general contractor, that causes so much unnecessary suffering. They deconstruct pain back to its true nature, returning you to the no-thingness, or emptiness, of pain. By becoming one with your pain, you're left with nothing to grasp. Your pain is gone—and so are you. What remains is an immaculate perception of pain, emptied of any level of contraction, reification, and therefore duality—and offering a glimpse of your own empty nature. (In his acclaimed study of esoteric consciousness in the ancient world, Peter Kingsley writes, "Black holes out there in the universe are nothing compared to the black holes in our own past. Those holes are much more than ordinary gaps. They have the power to destroy our ideas about ourselves and bring us face to face with nothingness."[1])

The practices of open awareness and reverse meditation help you see that your locus of identity, which for most of us is ego-based, is created by an unconscious process that resembles echolocation. In the physical world, echolocation occurs when an animal, like a bat or a whale, emits sound waves that bounce off an object and echo back, providing information about the object's size, shape, and distance. In humans, a comparable process takes place psychologically, but in a way that reverses the signals: you are constantly sending your awareness out, pinging it off seemingly external phenomena, as a way to provide information about *your* size, shape, and location. This signaling is part of the pulsation that takes place as awareness expands and contracts. In a twisted bidirectional way, you are reifying your pain "out there" with the unconscious intent to reify your sense of self "in here."

You may argue that pain is not "out there," that it's as intimate a phenomenon as you can get. But our colloquialisms reveal otherwise when we say things like "I am feeling pain." If I am feeling "that," I can't be that. If it's "my pain," it can't be me. Your feeling of pain may not be as distant as that tree out there, but until you get to step 4 of the reverse meditations, the feeling is nonetheless still subtly out there, or objectified, and can therefore be used in psychological "echolocation." Indeed, the closer the pain, the more echo data it provides. Because of the bidirectional process, the intensity or solidity of the pain is directly proportional to the solidity of who is feeling it. That is, the more solid you make your pain, the more solid you make yourself.

We participate in this psychological echo chamber because for many people, *anything* is better than nothing. With unwanted experience, at least you have something to wrestle with. Reifying our pain therefore serves a perverse egoic function. Writing about the intersection of Buddhism and psychotherapy, Bruce Tift makes an observation that aligns with the central insight of reverse meditation: "When we actually recover what has been disowned"—consider this to be the emotional pain we don't want to fully feel and own up to—"and bring it into our immediate embodied experience"—which in terms of reverse meditation culminates with step 4, the yoking—"we begin to dissolve our sense of having an essential self. We discover that, *absent a central struggle*, we have no center to our life at all."[2] Like the empty center of the whirlpool, the center of your being is openness—vast openness.

By resisting and fighting your pain, you solidify both the experience and the experiencer. You constantly pinch yourself as a heightened way to feel yourself.

The revelation of your reifying tendencies occurs when you discover just how hard it is to dissolve completely into the unwanted feeling, and to become one with it. Ego doesn't want you to become one with the pain, because when that happens ego disappears. By opening 100 percent to the feeling, you're removing the flickering of reference—the contractions—that gives birth to the illusion that *you* are feeling the pain. The lightning-fast reference (the "echolocation") is what creates the struggle, and therefore the self. You can detect all this as you work with step 4 of the reverse meditations. You open to the pain, and try to unite with it, but then reflexively (defensively) contract. With each pulsation, you generate the heartbeat of the ego, and solidify your pain.

For the ego—our locus of identity—it's not just that anything is better than nothing, but even something *bad* is better than no-thing (or emptiness) because there is no place for personal identity when things get this open. Because its survival is based on having something to press against, or struggle with, the ego is aberrantly invested in keeping up the fight. Put another way, ego is exclusive identification with form, and the more solid the form, the more solid the ego. But ego falls away as practices of open awareness and reverse meditation take you from fully reified form (the solidity of your pain) into fully dereified formlessness (the emptiness of pain). When you deconstruct and dereify your pain, by immediate implication, you're simultaneously deconstructing and dereifying your very sense of self. So, an unconscious conflict of interest is in play when you imagine getting rid of your pain: part of you wants to get rid of it, but part of you does not. (This tends to be especially true of psychological duress, compared to physical pain.) Accordingly, if you want to blame someone for your agony or your ecstasy, you need only look in the mirror.

Ego is a drama queen that loves to wrestle with difficulties. It's so perversely entertaining, we even pay for it. When we go to the movies (or get lost in a riveting novel), we're paying to get swept away in all manner of emotional conflict. Soap operas, and real operas, continue to sell. You'll hear people complain that art movies, like *My Dinner with Andre*, are boring. Where's the beef? Where's the Sturm and Drang? The entertainment industry rakes in billions of dollars reiterating the dramas and tragedies we love to inflict upon ourselves. This industry is merely an external expression of the industrious ego, which loves to gorge on drama more than popcorn.

EGOLESS PAIN

Pain becomes truly "selfless" when we dissolve into it 100 percent. Paradoxically, that's when pain and anguish feel better—at the point when they become egoless, purified of the stain of self. David Loy writes of anguish that the only thing we need to do with it is to "develop the ability to dwell in it or rather *as* it; then the anguish, having nowhere else to direct itself, consumes the sense of self."[3]

Does that mean we really don't exist? Well, it means we don't exist in the manner in which we think we do. On a relative level, we cannot deny appearance. In an unexamined way, there is this thing called "pain," and the entity feeling it. But closer examination reveals that appearance is not in harmony with reality. On an absolute level, you do not exist, and neither does your pain.

Our unwillingness to be so empty-handed is another reason most people don't want to do these practices and contract against them: many people would rather be with pain than be with no-thing—and *be* no-thing. How about you: Are you invested in your misery, despite the mounting costs? Are you willing to give up your ego to be free of your pain and suffering?

For most of us, the inability to be with the openness, or emptiness, at the core of our being generates a "primordial distraction"—the fundamental avoidance strategy, inseparable from the primordial contraction, from which all secondary distractions arise as iterations. We contract away from this empty core and into superficial levels of our identity, consolidating our awareness at the surface of our being. We then spend our lives essentially working on our tan.

Contraction—our resistance to unwanted experience, to anything that threatens our sense of self—generates this primary pulling apart from reality, from the harsh noble truth that we don't exist. For the fully formed ego, formlessness (emptiness/openness) is just too much because it's *too little* (there's nothing there). It's akin to death. The ego therefore dis-tracts itself from this unbearable truth, with a primordial ripping apart from reality, which is recapitulated every single time we get distracted.[4]

We're invested in distraction—and good at it—because it keeps the ego alive. By contrast, resting in the present moment without distraction, which eventually drops you into the empty center of yourself, annihilates the ego. In other words, ego is embodied distraction, fully formed distraction. Infinite formless awareness gets distracted in, and then falsely identified with, finite form. So, when you end distraction, you end the ego. Having nowhere to go, writes Peter Kingsley, "[is] the ultimate terror for the mind. But if you can stay in this hell, with no way to the left or to the right or in front or behind, then you discover the peace of utter stillness."[5]

The narrative of contraction (and its immediate manifestation as distraction) helps us understand the more subtle dimensions of enlightenment, and the path that gets us there. On the deepest levels, we don't ever attain enlightenment; we simply cease to be contracted.

Enlightenment is often depicted in terms of cessation and negation (*nonduality, nirvāṇa, nirodha, nirvikalpa*, etc.) The nondual traditions ask, How can you attain something you already have? The only thing you can do is stop contracting. Open. Then you will realize that what you've been seeking has been right in front of you all along. The Indian master Tilopa described achieving this liberating cessation through the complete selflessness, or egolessness, of Mahāmudrā meditation:

When the mind is free of reference point [contraction]
This is Mahāmudrā;
To get to know this, and intimately
Is to reach enlightenment's heights.[6]

Mahāmudrā is complete selflessness, or egolessness, and getting to know it is facilitated by getting to know your pain intimately.

How can pain and hardship facilitate this discovery? Pain and other unwanted experiences amplify samsāra—they heighten your samsāric tendency to pull apart from what's happening. Stop pulling apart from things, and you'll end the divorce proceedings against reality—you'll stop separating yourself from nirvāṇa. Pain magnifies your distractive/contractive tendencies, and therefore the opportunity to examine and transform the contractions. Indeed, great meditators learn to savor hardship rather than avoid it, because pain provides a heightened opportunity to *accelerate* the spiritual path. "Approach all that you find repulsive!" proclaimed Padampa Sangey. The greater the samsāra, the greater the opportunity to realize nirvāṇa.

When His Holiness the Sixteenth Karmapa was dying from cancer in an Illinois hospital, doctors and nurses checked with him daily and asked about his level of pain. He always replied, "No pain," and then inquired about how his caregivers were doing. His responses baffled the caretakers, who knew how painful his cancer was. When I was writing my book *Preparing to Die*, I interviewed several dozen meditation masters, including Tenga Rinpoche. When I was admitted to his quarters in Nepal, I was taken aback at his physical condition (he died several months after this visit). His body was a wreck. Diabetes had ravaged his limbs; he was nearly blind, confined to a wheelchair, and had to be hurting. I felt guilty being there and asked his attendants if I should leave. But Tenga Rinpoche greeted me warmly, with a beaming smile and playful demeanor. His relationship to his ransacked body made sense only after I learned about the reverse meditations. There was part of him that was completely untouched by his physical condition. He couldn't have cared less about his fading tan.

SUPPORT FROM HINDU NONDUAL TRADITIONS

Advaita Vedanta is the nondual school of the Hindu Vedanta tradition (one of the world's most ancient spiritualities), and the discipline teaches a process of deconstruction that has useful parallels with the four steps of reverse meditation. One of Advaita's modern exponents, the English spiritual teacher Rupert Spira, explained the nondual process of purifying a difficult emotion—and returning to pure perception—during a recent podcast:

> Let's take a feeling, like "I'm sad." In the Vedāntic approach, we explore the "I," the experiencer. We ignore the sadness, turn away from the sadness, and inquire, "Who is the I, or self, that is sad?" We turn away from the content and towards ourselves. The other approach, which is more tantric in spirit, is more inclusive. Here you turn towards the content, the feeling, and neglect the feeler, the "I." In this approach we turn toward the sadness and embrace it. We welcome it, we bring it close. And if we bring it so close that there is absolutely no resistance to it, then what would be left of the sadness if we no longer resisted it? There would no longer be any suffering. There would no longer be sadness as such.[7]

Is there a way to engage both these approaches simultaneously, as suggested in the four steps of reverse meditation? Spira teaches that there is such a way. He asks, "Can you step back away from the feeling, and at the same time lean into it and embrace it? The point is to forget the 'I' and to forget the sadness. What are you left with? Just the feeling. There is no self that is feeling it, there is no emotion being felt; there is just pure feeling." The sense of self, and the emotion, are both deconstructed, and one is left with pure perception.

Backing away from the feeling is equivalent to step 1 of the reverse meditations, whereas leaning in is equivalent to steps 2 through 4. "Instead of saying to yourself, 'I feel sad,'" he says, "take away the subject and the object, and just experience feeling. Don't experience the 'I,' don't experience the sadness, don't step away, don't go towards, just abide in the feeling."

This collapsing of subject and object into each other, the deconstruction of self and other, leads to nonduality. Or as Trungpa Rinpoche framed it, the absolute experience of duality *is* the experience of nonduality. Self and other, experience and experiencer, lean on each other. They *coemerge.* And if you pull either one away, they both collapse—into nonduality. Spira explains: "The separate subject of the experience and the separate object of the experience have no independent existence. The reality is pure feeling." That is, the subject and object are both empty of inherent existence, purified of self and other, subject and object. "Then you go a step further, and reduce pure feeling itself into knowing, consciousness, awareness." Here Advaita parallels the last step of open awareness, the awareness of awareness: "Because even feeling itself is a coloring of consciousness." He continues,

> In other words, feeling is not always present, but the stuff feeling is made of, pure knowing, or consciousness, is always present, and that's reality. Whichever of those three parts you take, whether it's the "I," or the contents of experience, or the feeling itself, you end up with pure consciousness.

Spira's "pure consciousness" is the equivalent of formless awareness. "Dispense with the subject and the object and go to pure seeing, hearing, or feeling; go to the essence of that experience, and you'll end up with pure knowing, or consciousness," he advises. "Whichever of those three pathways you take, you end up with reality."

In Advaita as in the reverse meditations, we come to the understanding that pure perception is empty perception—empty of perceiver and perceived. To reify is to stain; to dereify is to purify. Dereification (emptiness/nonduality) liberates the subject of the pain, the object that is the pain, and the very feeling of pain. So *who* is feeling *what*? You are not experiencing the pain; the pain is experiencing itself. Awareness is aware of itself.

"In a final sense, we don't exist," says Trungpa Rinpoche, teaching from the Tibetan tradition about the liberated (and fundamental) state of nonexistence: "We begin to realize that there is no one to even experience pain." Likewise,

> When we talk about emptiness, or the nonexistence of ego, we are speaking in terms of no ground to sit on. . . . Nobody's experiencing. Experience is just itself, it does not have any belongings. The experience also doesn't belong to you or to anybody else. It is just experience, and you choose it as yours and label it. But since there is no such thing as you, you don't experience anything. This is the whole point.[8]

Rinpoche then extends these nondual principles into the experience of enlightenment itself. In other words, you can use your new experience of enlightened pain to gain insights into enlightenment itself:

> In fact, you don't attain enlightenment—when you attain enlightenment there's no you left. So "you," as such, cannot attain enlightenment. You have to be disillusioned, dissolved, and then the attainment of enlightenment is there. I'm afraid it's rather hopeless. You can't witness the death of your own ego. You can't watch your own funeral.[9]

The whirlpool has to dissolve in order to enter the stream.

Another nondual tradition in Hinduism, Kashmir Shaivism, likewise has parallels with the four steps of reverse meditation. The rich lineage of Kashmir Shaivism emphasizes the importance of *turīya*, which translates as "the fourth" but has a meaning that is beyond words. Turīya is understood as that which is beyond the three common states of waking, dreaming, and dreamless sleep; it is the ineffable domain of absolute consciousness—beyond thought, beyond causality, beyond space and time, beyond any identification with the body or form altogether.

Faced with such concepts, the wisdom traditions once again depend on talking more about what reality is *not* rather than attempting to describe what it is—that is, whatever you can say about it is not it. We see an example in one of the core teachings of Vedānta—the *Māṇḍūkya-Upaniṣhad*—as that text describes the various states of consciousness and introduces turīya thus:

> (Turīya is) not that which cognizes the internal (objects), not that which cognizes the external (objects), not what cognizes both of them, not a mass of cognition, not cognitive, not non-cognitive. (It is) unseen, incapable of being spoken of, ungraspable, without any distinctive marks, unthinkable, unnamable, the essence of the knowledge of the one self, that into which the world is resolved, the peaceful, the benign.[10]

In terms of negation, turīya is "neither subjective nor objective experience, neither knowledge of the senses, nor relative knowledge, nor derived knowledge." In positive terms, it is "pure unified consciousness, unspeakable peace."[11] In some traditions, turīya is the highest state, the absolute witness. It's regarded as the only state unsoiled by the messy world of manifestation.

If one isn't careful, however, the doctrine that elevates turīya can easily take on the character of spiritual bypassing, accompanied by all the problems of absolutism. When turīya is misunderstood in this escapist way, instead of "transcend and include," your spiritual approach can slide into "transcend but exclude." Your spirituality then becomes elitist, exceptional, and disembodied. Because of these escapist inclinations, other traditions say there's one more step beyond turīya.

This highest state—turiyātīta ("beyond the fourth")—avoids the potential trap of spiritual bypassing by pulling a U-turn, bringing formless awareness back into the world of form. Turiyātīta invites the practitioner to infuse turīya, the transcendent witness, into all states: waking, dreaming, and dreamless sleep.[12] You go smack into the messy and limited manifestations, but now with the illuminating light of nondual awareness. Zvi Ish-Shalom lends a hand from the Jewish tradition: "There is no way for us to remove ourselves from the infinite nature of reality, regardless of how contracted and alienated from the source we may experience ourselves to be."[13]

Turiyātīta is not a fifth state, but an infusion of the fourth with all states. Christopher Wallis describes turiyātīta as "transcendence followed by pervasion of the mundane by the transcendent." The implication is that

> it is possible to experience the supreme Light of the Divine in the midst of any and all activities, and even in the midst of any and all moods or states of mind. To be more accurate, in this state we do not experience the Light *in spite* of our mood or condition or activity but *as the very substance* of those.[14]

"Beyond the fourth" really means "within the other three"—finding the spiritual in the material. "Ultimate Reality is simultaneously transcendent and immanent," in Wallis's words. In this vein, every morning I recite a liturgy that says, "Grant your blessings so that I realize the inseparability of samsāra and nirvāṇa." Grant your blessings so that I find peace in the midst of pain. The reverse meditations are a way to find that peace.

CONCLUSION

We've come a long way, and crossed a number of formidable hurdles, to arrive at the beginning—the start of a new way to work with unwanted experiences. We've challenged deeply ingrained views about the nature of reality: that it's not degraded and profane, but divine and sacred. We've worked to radically alter a lifetime of conditioning: instead of reflexively escaping from hardship, we're invited to plunge into it. And we've labored to overcome the most powerful of all habits: replacing contraction with openness.

It is not an easy journey. But neither is an authentic life. So be kind and gentle to yourself as you explore this heretical material. Take your time as you become familiar with something so unfamiliar. And test these teachings against your own experience. See if the four steps of the reverse meditations work for you. You may well find, as I have, that after some trial and error these practices are one of the greatest gifts you can give to yourself when things start to hurt.

Now that you have the tools, go out there and use them. And remember to smile. Smile at your pain, your fear, your heartache, with the look of inner confidence and freedom that comes from knowing you can handle anything that life throws your way.

ACKNOWLEDGMENTS

A deep bow of gratitude to Deborah Boyar, Candida Maurer, and Michael Taft for their insightful comments on the manuscript. A warm thank you to Tami Simon for her continued trust and confidence in me, and to Anastasia Pellouchoud for guiding this book to completion. Gretchen Gordon went beyond the call of duty with her editorial skills to craft this book into its final form. And Cindy Wilson provided the selfless thread that kept everything together. This book would not be here without her support.

NOTES

INTRODUCTION

1. Tibetan Buddhism comprises four traditions: One is the original school, based in the Nyingma, or "old translation," tradition. The other three schools are based in the Sarma, or "new translation," tradition—these are the Kagyu, Sakya, and Gelug schools. Mahāmudrā is a staple in the Sarma tradition. These four schools are further distinguished in that the Kagyu and Nyingma are considered "practice lineages"—that is, lineages that emphasize meditation—while the Gelug and Sakya are "scholastic lineages," which emphasize study. While I am a student of all four schools, my main path has been in the Kagyu and Nyingma traditions.

2. A. H. Almaas, *Facets of Unity: The Enneagram of Holy Ideas* (Boston: Shambhala, 2000), 54.

3. "The Eighteen Kinds of Yogic Joy," by Milarepa, translated and arranged by Jim Scott, in *Songs of Realization: As Taught & Sung by Khenchen Tsultrim Gyamtso Rinpoche* (Seattle: Nalandabodhi, 2013), 35.

4. Henry David Thoreau, *Walden and Civil Disobedience: Or, Life in the Woods* (New York: Signet Classics, 1999), 74.

5. Zvi Ish-Shalom, *The Kedumah Experience: The Primordial Torah* (Boulder: Albion-Andalus Books, 2017), 21. This description of the genesis of form is resonant with the *bardo* ["gap, transitional process, in between"] teachings of Tibetan Buddhism. From the radiance of the *luminous bardo of dharmata* we contract into the *karmic bardo of becoming*, and eventually into the *bardo of this life*, which occurs when the contractions of our mother physically reiterate this cosmological principle and literally squeeze us out into the world of form. We then reiterate this process throughout our lives every single time we grasp after something.

6. Ish-Shalom, *The Kedumah Experience: The Primordial Torah*, 39, 43.

7. See my book *Preparing to Die: Practical Advice and Spiritual Wisdom from the Tibetan Buddhist Tradition* (Boulder: Snow Lion, 2013); and

my first book, *The Power and the Pain: Transforming Spiritual Hardship into Joy* (Ithaca: Snow Lion Publications, 2009).

CHAPTER 1

1. The eightfold path consists of right view, right intention, right speech, right conduct, right livelihood, right effort, right mindfulness, right concentration.

2. Jill Bolte Taylor, *My Stroke of Insight: A Brain Scientist's Personal Journey* (New York: Plume, 2009), 72-74.

3. Carolyn Rose Gimian, ed., *The Collected Works of Chögyam Trungpa, Volume One* (Boston: Shambhala Publications, 2003), 462-63. See also *Pure Appearance*, and *Primordial Purity*, by Dilgo Khyentse Rinpoche.

4. Jeremy Hayward and Karen Hayward, *Sacred World: A Guide to Shambhala Warriorship in Everyday Life* (Boston: Shambhala Publications, 1995), 5-7.

5. Christopher D. Wallis, *The Recognition Sutras: Illuminating a 1,000-Year-Old Spiritual Masterpiece* (Boulder: Mattamayūra Press, 2017), 269.

6. Fung Yu-lan, trans., *Chuang-Tzu* (New York: Gordon Press, 1975), 53.

7. Mark S. G. Dyczkowski, *The Doctrine of Vibration: An Analysis of the Doctrines and Practices of Kashmir Shaivism* (Albany: State University of New York Press, 1987), 194.

8. Elaine Pagels, *The Gnostic Gospels* (New York: Vintage Books, 1979), 128-129.

9. Pagels, *The Gnostic Gospels*, 134, 139.

10. Personal correspondence, August 21, 2020.

11. A. H. Almaas, *Facets of Unity: The Enneagram of Holy Ideas* (Boston: Shambhala, 2000), 57-58.

12. Almaas, *Facets of Unity: The Enneagram of Holy Ideas*, 62-63.

13. Zvi Ish-Shalom, *The Kedumah Experience: The Primordial Torah* (Boulder: Albion-Andalus Books, 2017), 90.

14. Ish-Shalom, *The Kedumah Experience: The Primordial Torah*, 175.

15. Gimian, *The Collected Works of Chögyam Trungpa, Volume One*, 463.

16. Nishida Kitaro, *A Study of Good*, trans. V. H. Viglielmo (Japanese Government Printing Bureau, 1960), 48-49.

17. Sanskrit is replete with negating terms such as *nirvāṇa, nirodha, nirguna, nirvikalpa, niṣprapañca*. The West emphasizes the *Apophatic Way* (negative theology); and the East, the *Via Negativa* (the path of negation). As Meister Eckhart said, "The soul does not grow by addition but by subtraction."

18. Jack Kornfield, *A Path with Heart: A Guide Through the Perils and Promises of Spiritual Life* (New York: Bantam Books, 1993), 202.

19. Carlo Rovelli, *Helgoland: Making Sense of the Quantum Revolution* (New York: Riverhead Books, 2021), 75, 77, 79.

20. Anthony Aguirre, *Cosmological Koans: A Journey to the Heart of Physical Reality* (New York: W.W. Norton, 2019), 317.

21. Peter Kingsley, *In the Dark Places of Wisdom* (Point Reyes: The Golden Sufi Center, 2019), 34-35, 67.

22. Joseph Campbell with Bill Moyers, *The Power of Myth* (New York: Doubleday, 1998), 3.

CHAPTER 2

1. Daniel Maguire, *Ethics for a Small Planet*, in *Ecodharma: Buddhist Teachings for the Ecological Crises*, by David R. Loy (Somerville: Wisdom Publications, 2018), 37.

2. Raymond B. Blakney, trans. and ed., *Meister Eckhart: A Modern Translation* (Kila, MT: Kessinger, 2004), 127.

3. In the Tibetan Buddhist bardo teachings on death and dying, it is said that there are three levels of highest practitioner: (1) those who look forward to death, because they realize this greatest obstacle is really a once-in-a-lifetime opportunity; (2) those who have no fear of death, because they understand what death truly is; and (3) those who have no regrets, because they have lived life fully and fearlessly. The meditation master Gotsangpa sang, "When it's time to leave this body this, illusionary tangle / Don't cause yourself anxiety and grief / . . . / When mind forsakes the body, sheer delight!" Translated by Jim Scott and Anne Buchardi, ktgrinpoche.org/songs/seven-delights.

4. Carolyn Rose Gimian, ed., *The Collected Works of Chögyam Trungpa, Volume One* (Boston: Shambhala Publications, 2003), 461 2.

5. David R. Loy, *Ecodharma: Buddhist Teachings for the Ecological Crises* (Somerville: Wisdom Publications, 2018), 35.

6. David R. Loy, *Awareness Bound and Unbound: Buddhist Essays* (Albany: SUNY Press, 2009), 168-9.

7. Mircea Eliade, *The Sacred and the Profane: The Nature of Religion*, trans. Willard R. Trask (New York: Houghton Mifflin Harcourt, 1957), 12.

8. Eliade, *The Sacred and the Profane: The Nature of Religion*, 14.

9. Eliade, *The Sacred and the Profane: The Nature of Religion*, 25.

10. David R. Loy, *Nonduality: In Buddhism and Beyond* (Somerville: Wisdom Publications, 1988), 320.

11. Eliade, *The Sacred and the Profane: The Nature of Religion*, 28.

12. Vanessa Zuisei Goddard, "The Places We Go to Be Here," *Tricycle Magazine*, Summer 2020, tricycle.org/magazine/sacred-spaces/.

13. Multiple personality disorder, or dissociative identity disorder, is one extreme example of this attempt to escape. When a person is experiencing extreme distress, the mind can dissociate to such an extent that sub-personalities are generated.

14. Lesser Jihad is what we know as more traditional forms of "holy war," where the enemy is projected to be external.

15. Chögyam Trungpa and Francesca Fremantle, trans., *The Tibetan Book of the Dead* (Boston: Shambhala Publications, 1975), 3. Emphasis added.

CHAPTER 3

1. Zvi Ish-Shalom, *The Path of Primordial Light: Ancient Wisdom for the Here and Now* (Sioux Falls: Light Beacon Press, 2022), 112.

CHAPTER 4

1. Andrew Holecek, "Bernardo Kastrup, Part 1: A Rich Exploration of Idealism," *The Edge of Mind* podcast, July 11, 2022. edgeofmindpodcast.com/bernardo-kastrup-part-i-a-rich-exploration-of-idealism/.

2. In Buddhism, these three states relate to the formless *dharmakāya* ("truth body"), the partially formed *sambhogakāya* ("bliss body"), and the fully formed *nirmānakāya* ("emanation body"). Daytime practices that introduce you to, and allow you to become familiar with, the formless dimensions include Dzogchen and Mahāmudrā, from the Tibetan tradition, and the practices of Advaita Vedānta and Nondual Shaiva Tantra, from Hinduism. The nocturnal meditation of sleep yoga (or luminosity yoga) also cultivates this recognition of formless awareness, and the ability to attain lucidity, or awareness, in deep sleep.

   Clark Strand writes: "Turn out the lights—and leave them off—and we will experience a consciousness our minds have never known but our bodies still remember . . . We can't find our souls in the daylight, since we lost them in the night . . . Turn out the lights and leave them off and, in short, you remember who you are." Clark Strand, *Waking up to the Dark: Ancient Wisdom for a Sleepless Age* (New York: Spiegel & Grau, 2015), 53-54.

3. Matthew Walker, *Why We Sleep: Unlocking the Power of Sleep and Dreams* (New York: Scribner, 2017), 57. Causal consciousness is deeply connected to the Hindu description of turīya, which we will explore in chapter 13.

4. A landmark study by the psychobiologist Thomas Wehr suggests that even our sleep patterns have contracted. Prior to the advent of artificial light, sleep was segmented or bi-phasic, meaning our ancestors slept "the first sleep" for about four hours, woke up some two hours (the "Hour of God"), then fell back for "the second sleep." Wehr writes, "It is tempting to speculate that in prehistoric times this arrangement provided a channel of communication between dreams and waking life that has gradually been closed off as humans have compressed and consolidated their sleep. If so, then this alteration [and alienation] might provide a physiological explanation for the observation that modern humans seem to have lost touch with the wellspring of myths and fantasies." Thomas A. Wehr, "In short photoperiods, human sleep is biphasic," *Journal of Sleep Research*, Volume 1, Issue 2 (June 1992): 103-107. onlinelibrary.wiley.com/doi/10.1111/j.1365-2869 .1992.tb00019.x See also: A. Roger Ekirch, *At Day's Close: Night in Times Past*; Jane Brox, *Brilliant: The Evolution of Artificial Light*; and Christopher Dewdney, *Acquainted with the Night: Excursions Through the World After Dark*.

5. Reginald A. Ray, *Somatic Descent: How to Unlock the Deepest Wisdom of the Body* (Boulder: Shambhala Publications, 2020), 121.

6. This entire journey of the contraction into form is discussed as *involution* by writers like Sri Aurobindo, Gurdjieff, and Ken Wilber. Involution is then reversed in the journey of *evolution*, or the return of form into the formless, a cyclic process that takes place not just when we fall asleep and wake up, but at universal levels. Plotinus, in the *Enneads*, discussed it in terms of *emanation* (or *efflux*, clearly connected to the "emanation body," or *nirmāṇakāya*, in Buddhism). Here, too, the process is reversed by *epostrophē*, or "reversion" (*reflux*). Jewish and Arabic philosophers also ran with these principles.

7. Liminal dreaming is a neologism for the hypnogogic state, the plasma of mind when you transition from the waking state into sleep. See my books *Dream Yoga, Dreams of Light*, and *The Lucid Dreaming Workbook*. Or Jennifer Dumpert, *Liminal Dreaming: Exploring Consciousness at the Edges of Sleep* (Berkeley: North Atlantic Books, 2019).

8. Lucid sleeping is maintaining awareness in deep, dreamless sleep. Referred to as *minimal phenomenal experience* (MPE) in the scientific community, it is currently being studied in a number of labs around the world. The philosopher Thomas Metzinger asserts that when MPE is proven, it will be a revolution in the mind sciences.

9. The other realms being the *realm of form* and the *formless realms*. These realms are entered, psychologically and ontologically (they are as real, or unreal, as the realm of form), through deep meditative absorption.

CHAPTER 5

1. *Is Everything Made of Matter or Consciousness? Rupert Spira and Bernardo Kastrup in Conversation*, Youtube, accessed April 19, 2022, youtube.com/watch?v=MQuMzocvmTQ.

2. The bardo teachings are deeply connected to the teachings on emptiness. In short, we take on existence because we believe in existence; we take on a body after death because we believe we're somebody.

3. Reginald A. Ray, *The Awakening Body: Somatic Meditation for Discovering Our Deepest Life* (Boulder, CO: Shambhala Publications, 2016), 41.

4. "More than 60 percent of the people on the planet and fully 99 percent in the United States and Europe exist under a yellowy lit-up night sky; Light emissions have been rising an average rate of 2.2 percent each year since 2012, with emissions growing in some regions as much as 20 percent; The 100-watt light bulb, left on every night for a year, is powered by the equivalent of a half-ton of coal; Nocturnal animals make up 30 percent of all vertebrates and 60 percent of all invertebrates, and their health has been severely threatened; In 2019, researchers reported that West Nile-virus–infected house sparrows inhabiting light-polluted areas were infectious for two days longer than those birds living in darkness. This increased the risk of a West Nile outbreak by 21 percent." Deborah Eden Tull, *Luminous Darkness: An Engaged Buddhist Approach to Embracing the Unknown, A Path to Personal and Collective Awakening* (Boulder: Shambhala, 2022), 35-36.

5. "Let us take time . . . to be bored, to strip away from ourselves the screens we have created to hide the real truths of life and death from our eyes." Carl Trueman, *The Wages of Spin* (Ross-shire, Scotland: Mentor, 2007), 179-80.

CHAPTER 6

1. Reginald A. Ray, *The Awakening Body: Somatic Meditation for Discovering Our Deepest Life* (Boulder: Shambhala, 2016), 41-42.

2. Ruben E. Laukkonen and Heleen A. Slagter, "From many to (n)one: Meditation and the plasticity of the predictive mind," *Neuroscience & Biobehavioral Reviews*, Vol 128 (Sept 2021): 199-217.

3. Carlo Rovelli, *Helgoland: Making Sense of the Quantum Revolution* (New York: Riverhead Books, 2021), 193-95.

4. Hippolyte Taine, *De l'intelligence*, in Rovelli, *Helgoland*, 195.

5. Deborah Eden Tull, *Luminous Darkness: An Engaged Buddhist Approach to Embracing the Unknown* (Boulder: Shambhala, 2022), 73.

6. The wind analogy takes on meaning in the inner yogas (sometimes called "wind yoga"), which deal with the subtle inner body. One of the major players in subtle body yoga is "wind," or *prana* in Sanskrit, *lung* in Tibetan, and *chi* in Chinese. It's considered the most powerful of all the elements. In the Kalachakra Tantra, the "King of all Tantras," it is said that wind is what creates and destroys individual and collective

world systems. Meditation in general, and the inner yogas in particular, is the art of unwinding (un-winding) all the contractions. This imbues the practitioner with incredible energy.

7. Bernardo Kastrup, *Why Materialism is Baloney: How true skeptics know there is no death and fathom answers to life, the universe, and everything* (Hampshire, UK: Iff Books, 2014), 81. The whirlpool image also dovetails in the twelve *nidanas*, or links of dependent origination, that continually cycle to generate samsara in the Buddhist view.

8. Kastrup, *Why Materialism is Baloney*, 182-83.

9. The other three being "once-returner," "non-returner," and "worthy one" or Arhat. The idea of "entering the stream" is also connected to the Vajrayāna notion of "entering the action."

10. The other two being: cutting doubt in the teachings and cutting attachment to rites and rituals.

11. Evan Thompson, *Waking, Dreaming, Being: Self and Consciousness in Neuroscience, Meditation, and Philosophy* (New York: Columbia University Press, 2015), 44.

CHAPTER 7

1. Vanessa Zuisei Goddard, "The Places We Go to Be Here," *Tricycle Magazine*, Summer 2020, tricycle.org/magazine/sacred-spaces/.

2. Chögyam Trungpa Rinpoche, *The Dathun Letter*, accessed April 22, 2022, chronicleproject.com/the-dathun-letter/.

3. The economy of the ego starts right here, as does every form of consumerism. In the untamed mind, every thought advertises "grasp me, contract around me." "Come with me, and I'll set you free" from the banality of the present moment.

4. David R. Loy, *Awareness Bound and Unbound: Buddhist Essays* (Albany: State University of New York Press, 2009), 100.

5. Stopping and sitting is *shamatha*. The ability to see, gained through insight practice is *vipashyana*. The practice of meditation described in this chapter is therefore more accurately called *referential shamatha-vipashyana*.

6. In an innovative set of studies, Arthur Deikman suggested the plausibility of penetrating through dualistic perception and into

nondual vision, concluding: "If, as evidence indicates, our passage from infancy to adulthood is accompanied by an organization of the perceptual and cognitive world that has as its price the selection of some stimuli to the exclusion of others, it is quite possible that a technique could be found to *reverse* or undo, temporarily, the automatization that has restricted our communication with reality to the active perception of only a small segment of it. Such a process of de-automatization might then be followed by an awareness of aspects of reality that were formerly unavailable to us." [Emphasis added.] Arthur J. Deikman, MD, "Implications of Experimentally Induced Contemplative Meditation," *Journal of Nervous and Mental Disease*, Vol 142, Issue 2 (February 1966): 101-116. journals.lww.com/jonmd /citation/1966/02000/implications_of_experimentally_induced.1.aspx.

7. Goddard, "The Places We Go to Be Here."

8. Goddard, "The Places We Go to Be Here." Emphasis added.

CHAPTER 8

1. The referential meditations are akin to the Centering Prayer that derives from the Desert Fathers, a prayer that gathers and silences the mind, while the nonreferential meditations are like a decentering prayer. Once the mind is collected and settled, we open it. Centering is a healthy form of contraction, engaging the etymology of *con-tract* as to "draw together." When we get ourselves together, we can relax and allow ourselves to come apart.

2. In the language of yogachara Buddhism, open awareness brings the unconscious workings of the seventh consciousness (*klista manas*) into the light of consciousness, eventually transforming it into the wisdom of equality. This is something you can feel in your practice, as the stickiness of the mind, and the constant reference back to self, are replaced with equanimity, and radical acceptance toward whatever arises.

3. From a purely psychological perspective, Carl Jung knew this, and expanded upon it with his teachings on "individuation."

4. David R. Loy, *Awareness Bound and Unbound: Buddhist Essays*, (Albany: State University of New York Press, 2009), 15.

5. B. Alan Wallace, *Dreaming Yourself Awake: Lucid Dreaming and Tibetan Dream Yoga for Insight and Transformation* (Boston: Shambhala Publications, 2012), 60-61.

CHAPTER 9

1. David R. Loy, *Lack & Transcendence: The Problem of Death and Life in Psychotherapy, Existentialism, and Buddhism* (Sommerville: Wisdom Publications, 2018), 169.

2. David R. Loy, *Lack & Transcendence*, 171.

3. David R. Loy, *Lack & Transcendence*, 173.

4. Daniel Goleman and Richard Davidson, *Altered Traits: Science Reveals How Meditation Changes Your Mind, Brain, and Body* (New York: Avery, 2017), 162-63.

5. Rupert Spira, *The Nature of Consciousness: Essays on the Unity of Mind and Matter* (Oxford: Sahaja Publications, 2017), 183.

6. When the Hubble was first launched, and the telescope opened its eyes, the first images were a colossal disappointment. As engineers scrambled to figure out what happened, they discovered that the reflecting mirrors were not polished properly, creating all manner of optical distortions. It took one of the most heroic rescue missions in the history of science to repair this problem, which resulted in the mind-expanding images we now celebrate as the gift of Hubble.

7. Bernardo Kastrup, *Science Ideated: The fall of matter and the contours of the next mainstream scientific world view* (Winchester, UK: Iff books, 2020), 46-47.

8. A more dramatic analogy brings us back to the Hubble. Astronomers wanted to use the telescope to estimate how many stars are in the universe. They focused the lens of the Hubble on a black dot in space, the size of a drinking straw. Over the course of ten days, the "gaze" remained fixed on this pitch-black dot. Points of light started to emerge, and eventually some ten thousand points of light were detected in this tiny space. It turned out that each point wasn't just a star, but an undetected *galaxy*, containing between 100 to 200 billion stars! Scientists then estimated that there are more stars in the known universe (which only gets bigger the more they look) than there are grains of sand on every beach on Earth.

9. Transcript from a talk given by Khenpo Tsültrim Gyamtso Rinpoche, commentary on the text *Essential Points of Creation and Completion*, by

Jamgön Kongtrul Lodrö Thaye, at Karma Dzong, Boulder, CO, June 1996, Talk 7, translated by Sarah Harding, p. 61.

10. Jamgön Kongtrul, *Creation and Completion: Essential Points of Tantric Meditation*, trans. Sarah Harding (Boston: Wisdom Publications, 2002), 130.

CHAPTER 10

1. Ian Baker, *The Heart of the World: A Journey to Tibet's Lost Paradise* (London: Thames Hudson, 2020), 240.

2. One classification of all the Buddha's teachings comes in the form of the *three yānas*, or "vehicles": tantra is synonymous with the *Vajrayāna*, or "diamond vehicle"; *Mahāyāna* is the "great" or "wide vehicle"; and *Hinayāna* is the "individual" or "narrow vehicle."

3. Pema Chödrön, *Tonglen: The Path of Transformation* (Halifax: Vajradhatu Publications, 2001).

4. Reginald R. Ray, *Somatic Descent: How to Unlock the Deepest Wisdom of the Body* (Boulder: Shambhala, 2020), 126.

5. Robert Augustus Masters, *Spiritual Bypassing: When Spirituality Disconnects Us from What Really Matters* (Berkeley: North Atlantic Books, 2010), 3.

6. Masters, *Spiritual Bypassing*, 3.

7. Masters, *Spiritual Bypassing*, 5.

8. Joseph Campbell's famous maxim "Follow your bliss!" certainly has provisional validity. But if you only follow your bliss, you'll just get blissed out of reality. If you really want to grow, try balancing that with "follow your fear," or some other variant of "follow your discomfort plan."

9. Masters, *Spiritual Bypassing*, 13.

10. Scott Barry Kaufman, "The Science of Spiritual Narcissism," in *Scientific American*, January 11, 2021, scientificamerican.com/article/the-science-of-spiritual-narcissism/.

11. Kaufman continues: "Healthy transcendence is not about being outside of the whole, or feeling superior to the whole, but being

a harmonious part of the whole of human existence. . . . Healthy transcendence involves harnessing all that you are in the service of realizing the best version of yourself so you can help raise the bar for the whole of humanity." The challenge, then, is to find the harmony in dissonance, realizing that dissonant aspects of life have a rightful place in the modern symphony that is our life. Kaufman, "The Science of Spiritual Narcissism."

12. Masters, *Spiritual Bypassing*. Emphasis added.

13. Bruce Tift, *Already Free: Buddhism Meets Psychotherapy on the Path of Liberation* (Boulder: Sounds True, 2015), 46.

14. Tift, *Already Free*, 46.

15. The spirit of the reverse meditations is resonant with Jon Kabat-Zinn's mindfulness-based stress reduction (MBSR) programs, but more intense and profound. See Jon Kabat-Zinn, *Full Catastrophe Living: Using the Wisdom of Your Body and Mind to Face Stress, Pain, and Illness* (New York: Bantam Books, 2013). For more on MBSR, see Daniel Goleman and Richard J. Davidson, *Altered Traits: Science Reveals How Meditation Changes Your Mind, Brain, and Body* (London: Viking, 2017), 165-190.

16. Chögyam Trunpga, *The Myth of Freedom; and the Way of Meditation*, eds. John Baker and Marvin Casper (Boston: Shambhala, 1988), 73-74.

17. Masters, *Spiritual Bypassing*, 19.

18. Masters, *Spiritual Bypassing*, 19-20.

19. Christopher D. Wallis, *Tantra Illuminated: The Philosophy, History, and Practice of a Timeless Tradition* (Boulder: Mattamayūra Press, 2013), 362-63.

20. Wallis, *Tantra Illuminated*, 362-63.

21. This principle is engaged in instruments like lie detectors, which listen more to body language than to literal language. Catastrophizing is when you assume that the worst will happen. You *think* you're in a worse situation than you really are; you exaggerate the difficulties. Confabulation is the fabrication of imaginary experiences, the endless storylines we weave and then get stuck in, like a spider getting snared in its own web. It's sometimes called "honest lying," because we

honestly just don't know that we're confabulating; we totally conflate and confuse the map (our thinking) with the territory (reality).

22. Christopher M. Bache, *LSD and the Mind of the Universe: Diamonds from Heaven* (Rochester: Park Street Press, 2019), 35-6.

23. Reginald A. Ray, *Touching Enlightenment: Finding Realization in the Body* (Boulder: Sounds True, 2008), 81.

24. The idea that your body is your personal earth implies that the way we relate to our body is the way we relate to the earth. The ecological crisis also begins right here, and is to be cured right here. By connecting to our body, and enhancing our relationship to it, we naturally extend that healthy internal relationship to the external planet. For more, see Ray, *Touching Enlightenment: Finding Realization in the Body*, 21-54. Also see David R. Loy, *Ecodharma: Buddhist Teachings for the Ecological Crises* (Somerville: Wisdom Publications, 2018).

25. Bache, *LSD and the Mind of the Universe: Diamonds from Heaven*, 37.

26. This is precisely what my three-year retreat felt like: a massive de-icing, which inspired me to write *The Power and the Pain: Transforming Spiritual Hardship into Joy* (Ithaca: Snow Lion Publications, 2010).

27. Ray, *Touching Enlightenment*, 8. Emphasis added.

28. Ray, *Touching Enlightenment*, 82.

29. Ray, *Touching Enlightenment*, 82.

30. Dark retreat is part of Tibetan and Bön Buddhism, as well as ancient Greek ritual. See Tenzin Wangyal, *Wonders of the Natural Mind: The Essence of Dzogchen in the Native Bon Tradition of Tibet* (New Delhi: New Age Books, 2004) and Yulia Ustinova, *Caves and the Ancient Greek Mind: Descending Underground in the Search for Ultimate Truth* (Oxford: Oxford University Press, 2009).

31. Tift, *Already Free*, 131-67.

32. Shunryu Suzuki, *Zen Mind, Beginner's Mind: Informal Talks on Zen Meditation and Practice* (New York: Weatherhill, 1985), 63.

33. By incinerating our experience as we live it, we put an end to karma, and the generation of the *samskaras*, or undigested energy patterns, which run most of our lives, and create further karma. See chapter 13.

Wallis writes, "The mental-emotional body (*puryastaka*) stores traces of those experiences in direct proportion to how incompletely they were digested at the time of occurrence." If you incinerate your experience as you live it, "then you are able to 'digest' that experience fully, which means allow all its energy to pass through your system without resistance." Christopher D. Wallis, *The Recognition Sutras: Illuminating a 1,000-Year-Old Spiritual Masterpiece* (Boulder: Mattamayūra Press, 2017), 302, 310.

34. Wallis, *The Recognition Sutras*, 237.

35. At the Center for Investigating Healthy Minds, in a study led by neuroscientist Richard J. Davidson.

36. Scientists also distinguish pain from nociception. Nociception is the physiological process by which we detect injury; pain is the secondary process that follows from that. Nociception correlates to the first of these three aspects, the sensory aspect. If I stub my toe, nociception occurs in my toe (and spinal cord); pain is produced by my brain. Nociception can be restricted to the peripheral nervous system; pain always involves the brain. In other words, nociception can occur without conscious awareness, but pain cannot. Centrifuging out the similarities and differences between scientific, psychological, and spiritual renderings of nociception, pain, and suffering is beyond our scope.

37. For how Tibetan Buddhist meditators fared in similar studies, see Perlman, Solomon, Davidson, and Lutz, "Differential Effects of Pain Intensity and Unpleasantness of Two Meditation Practices," *Emotion*, 10 (2010): 65-71; and Lutz, McFarlin, Perlman, Salomons, and Davidson, "Altered Anterior Insula Activation During Anticipating and Experience of Painful Stimuli in Expert Meditators," *Neuroimage*, 64 (2013): 538-46.

38. Evan Thompson, "Conceptualizing Cognition in Buddhist Philosophy and Cognitive Science" (presidential address delivered at the ninety-fifth Pacific Division meeting of the American Philosophical Association, April 9, 2021), 70.

39. J. A. Grant, "Meditative Analgesia: The Current Status of the Field," *Annals of the New York Academy of Sciences*, 1307 (2013): 55-63.

40. Thompson further articulates the benefits of the referential and nonreferential meditations: "Reducing affective and motivational biases of attention through mindfulness meditation

practices appears to alter perception, specifically the experienced unpleasantness of pain. Open monitoring meditation appears to attenuate the affect-biased attentional selection and attentional inhibition, affect-biased appraisal and anticipation, and approach-versus-avoid action tendencies. Accordingly, we can speculate that it may also weaken the subject-object structure of phenomenal intentionality." Evan Thompson, "Conceptualizing Cognition in Buddhist Philosophy and Cognitive Science" (presidential address delivered at the ninety-fifth Pacific Division meeting of the American Philosophical Association, April 9, 2021), 72-73.

CHAPTER 11

1. A recent study, summarized in this article where the title says it all, "People would rather be electrically shocked than left alone with their thoughts," showed that given the choice of being bored or in pain, many people (67 percent of men and 25 percent of women) preferred the pain. "I found it quite surprising and a bit disheartening that people seem to be so uncomfortable when left to their own devices; that they can be so bored that even being shocked seemed more entertaining," says Jonathan Schooler, a psychology professor. sciencemag.org/news/2014/07/people-would -rather-be-electrically-shocked-left-alone-their-thoughts. Accessed January 14, 2021.

2. Yongey Mingyur Rinpoche with Helen Tworkov, *In Love with the World: A Monk's Journey Through the Bardos of Living and Dying* (New York: Random House, 2019), 37.

3. On extreme levels, like an abused child trying to psychically survive an assault, the child may dissociate from the unwanted experience to such an extent that the result is dissociative identity disorder, formerly called multiple personality disorder. That is obviously not what we're trying to cultivate here.

4. Sam Harris, *Waking Up: A Guide to Spirituality Without Religion* (New York: Simon & Schuster, 2014), 137.

5. Ken Wilber, *No Boundary: Eastern and Western Approaches to Personal Growth* (Boston: Shambhala, 2001), 130-31.

6. Christopher D. Wallis, *The Recognition Sutras: Illuminating a 1,000-Year-Old Spiritual Masterpiece* (Boulder: Mattamayūra Press, 2017), 244.

7. Wallis, *The Recognition Sutras*, 249.

8. Ven. Khenpo Karthar Rinpoche, "A Commentary on The Ocean of True Meaning, Part 3" (transcript of the 1994 Ten Day Teachings), trans. Yeshe Gyamtso. (KTD Dharma Goods, 1995), 43.

9. Zvi Ish-Shalom, *The Path of Primordial Light: Ancient Wisdom for the Here and Now* (Sioux Falls: Light Beacon Press, 2022), 53-54.

10. Chögyam Trungpa and Francesca Fremantle, trans., *The Tibetan Book of the Dead* (Boston: Shambhala Publications, 1975), 3.

11. "The Dazzling Dark," an interview with John Wren-Lewis by Caroline Jones, Youtube, accessed September 14, 2022, youtube.com/watch?v=TDHsi-HOiQU.

12. Ngawang Zangpo, *Sacred Ground: Jamgön Kongtrül on "Pilgrimage and Sacred Geography"* (Ithaca: Snow Lion Publications, 2001), 38.

13. Yongey Mingyur Rinpoche, *In Love with the World: A Monk's Journey Through the Bardos of Living and Dying* (New York: Random House, 2021), 13.

14. *The Art of War* by Sun Tzu is a classic Chinese manual for working skillfully with any level of conflict. Lesser Jihad is what we hear about in the news.

15. Christopher D. Wallis, *Tantra Illuminated: The Philosophy, History, and Practice of a Timeless Tradition* (Boulder: Mattamayūra Press, 2013), 65.

16. Bruce H. Lipton, *The Biology of Belief: Unleashing the Power of Consciousness, Matter & Miracles* (Carlsbad: Hay House, Inc., 2016), 119.

CHAPTER 12

1. David R. Loy, *Nonduality: In Buddhism and Beyond* (Somerville: Wisdom Publications, 1988), 218.

2. Translated and arranged by Jim Scott, *Songs of Realization: As Taught & Sung by Khenchen Tsultrim Gyamtso Rinpoche* (Seattle: Nalandabodhi, 2013). This is my "desert island" book. The most concentrated and profound body of wisdom teachings ever collected in a single volume, and rendered in the form of songs.

3. The quote continues: "Eighty-five percent of the time we are magnificently equipped to heal ourselves. Never underestimate the body's power to heal." Norman Cousins, "Norman Cousins believes joy is cure for world's problems," interview by Don Adair, Spokane Chronicle, April 15th, 1983, news.google.com/newspapers?nid=1345 &dat=19830415&id=u88vAAAAIBAJ&sjid=mvkDAAAAIBAJ&pg= 4859,3563845.

4. I'm a private person, always hesitant to share my inner landscape. But the timing around this diagnosis, the flurry of appointments with surgeons, urologists, radiation oncologists, internal medicine specialists, just a few weeks before delivering this book about pain and suffering to my publisher, was too much to ignore. It felt disingenuous not to share what was happening, and my honest response to it all.

5. Christopher D. Wallis, *The Recognition Sutras: Illuminating a 1,000-Year-Old Spiritual Masterpiece* (Boulder: Mattamayūra Press, 2017), 247-48.

6. David R. Loy, *The Great Awakening: A Buddhist Social Theory* (Somerville: Wisdom Publications, 2003), 177.

7. Loy, *The Great Awakening*, 184.

8. As a member of the American Academy of Sleep Medicine, I often counseled patients about how to manage this number one sleep disorder (there are over 100 sleep disorders). Cognitive Behavioral Therapy for Insomnia, or CBTI, is perhaps the most frequently used, and successful, regimen. Seventy to eighty percent of patients report benefits. But this application of the reverse meditations is also highly effective, even though no formal studies support this claim.

9. Zvi Ish-Shalom, *The Path of Primordial Light: Ancient Wisdom for the Here and Now* (Sioux Falls: Light Beacon Press, 2022), 113.

CHAPTER 13

1. Peter Kingsley, *In the Dark Places of Wisdom* (Point Reyes: The Golden Sufi Center, 2019), 55.

2. Bruce Tift, *Already Free: Buddhism Meets Psychotherapy on the Path of Liberation* (Boulder: Sounds True, 2015), 139. Emphasis added.

3. David R. Loy, *Lack & Transcendence: The Problem of Death and Life in Psychotherapy, Existentialism, and Buddhism* (Sommerville: Wisdom Publications, 2018), 92.

4. In the bardo teachings of Tibetan Buddhism, it is our inability to be with the "bright lights," the blinding truth of the *luminous bardo of dharmata* ("isness, suchness, reality"), that generates the primordial distraction, or pulling-apart, that rips us away from the luminous emptiness revealed at death. This propels us into and through the karmic bardo of becoming, and eventually into the bardo of this life. This entire birthing process, from complete formlessness to fully reified form, is therefore a sophisticated avoidance strategy. Samsāra is therefore one massive, protracted, and (literally) embodied distraction. No wonder we're distracted all the time.

5. Kingsley, *In the Dark Places of Wisdom*, 35.

6. Khenpo Tsültrim Gyamtso Rinpoche (from a seminar given at Rocky Mountain Dharma Center, summer 1991), *Mahāmudrā, Shamatha, and Vipashyana*, trans. Jim Scott (Halifax: Vajravairochana Translation Committee, 1993), 46.

7. Robert Spira, Simon Mundie, and Jamie Robson, "From Suffering to Freedom," *Robert Spira Podcast*, December 28, 2021, youtube.com/watch?v=ajZHOptMo2I.

8. Chogyam Trungpa, *Cynicism and Magic: Intelligence and Intuition on the Buddhist Path*, ed. the Opening the Dharma Treasury Editors Group (Boulder: Shambhala, 2021), 15, 20.

9. Trungpa, *Cynicism and Magic: Intelligence and Intuition on the Buddhist Path*, 20.

10. S. Radhakrishnan, *The Principal Upaniṣads* (Great Britain: HarperCollins, 2009), 698.

11. *The Encyclopedia of Eastern Philosophy and Religion* (Boston: Shambhala Publications, 1989), 388.

12. A U-turn that is also a You-turn. One returns to manifest the wisdom of turīya as the compassion of turīyātīta. You come back to earth, to integrated reality, to help others. I'm coming back to help you. Many near-death experiences share this impulse. "What I experienced was beyond bliss, but it wasn't time for me to go. Something called me back to return to life." See Yongey Mingyur Rinpoche with Helen

Tworkov, *In Love with the World: A Monk's Journey Through the Bardos of Living and Dying* (New York: Random House, 2019), chapters 28–29, for one notable story.

13. Zvi Ish-Shalom, *The Path of Primordial Light: Ancient Wisdom for the Here and Now* (Sioux Falls: Light Beacon Press, 2022), 24.

14. Christopher D. Wallis, *Tantra Illuminated: The Philosophy, History, and Practice of a Timeless Tradition* (Boulder: Mattamayūra Press, 2013), 179-80.

ABOUT THE AUTHOR

Andrew Holecek is an author, speaker, and humanitarian who offers seminars internationally on meditation, lucid dreaming, and the art of dying. He is the author of many books, including *The Power and the Pain: Transforming Spiritual Hardship into Joy*, and *Preparing to Die: Practical Advice and Spiritual Wisdom from the Tibetan Buddhist Tradition*. Dr. Holecek is a member of the American Academy of Sleep Medicine, and the coauthor of scientific papers on lucid dreaming. His work has appeared in *Psychology Today*, *Parabola*, *Lion's Roar*, *Tricycle*, *Utne Reader*, *Buddhadharma*, *Light of Consciousness*, and many other periodicals. He also hosts the popular *Edge of Mind* podcast (edgeofmindpodcast.com), conversations with leading-edge thinkers in the fields of science, philosophy, spirituality, psychology, integral studies, and the arts. Andrew is the founder of the international Night Club community (nightclub.andrewholecek.com), a support platform for nocturnal meditations, and the co-founder of Global Dental Relief (globaldentalrelief.org), which provides free oral health care to children in developing countries. He holds degrees in classical music, biology, and a doctorate in dental surgery. Learn more at andrewholecek.com.

ABOUT SOUNDS TRUE

Sounds True is a multimedia publisher whose mission is to inspire and support personal transformation and spiritual awakening. Founded in 1985 and located in Boulder, Colorado, we work with many of the leading spiritual teachers, thinkers, healers, and visionary artists of our time. We strive with every title to preserve the essential "living wisdom" of the author or artist. It is our goal to create products that not only provide information to a reader or listener but also embody the quality of a wisdom transmission.

For those seeking genuine transformation, Sounds True is your trusted partner. At SoundsTrue.com you will find a wealth of free resources to support your journey, including exclusive weekly audio interviews, free downloads, interactive learning tools, and other special savings on all our titles.

To learn more, please visit SoundsTrue.com/freegifts or call us toll-free at 800.333.9185.